ANTOINE Plamondon

1804–1895 *Milestones of an Artistic Journey*

ANTOINE *Plamondon*

1804–1895 *Milestones of an Artistic Journey*

John R. Porter and Mario Béland

Musée national des beaux-arts du Québec

This publication is a catalogue for the *Antoine Plamondon (1804-1895).*
Milestones of an Artistic Journey exhibition organized by the
Musée national des beaux-arts du Québec and presented from
November 24, 2005, to April 9, 2006.

- Curators: John R. Porter, Executive Director, and Mario Béland,
  Curator of Early Québec Art, 1850 to 1900
- Project Director: Line Ouellet, Director of Exhibitions and Education
- General Coordinator: Mario Béland
- Exhibition Designer, Québec City: Denis Allison, Head Designer
- Touring Exhibition Coordinator: Louise Dubois

Musée national des beaux-arts du Québec
Parc des Champs-de-Bataille
Québec (Québec)
Canada G1R 5H3
Phone: (418) 643-2150
www.mnba.qc.ca

- Executive Director: John R. Porter
- Director of Collections and Research: Yves Lacasse
- Director of Exhibitions and Education: Line Ouellet
- Director of Administration and Communications: Marc Delaunay

PRODUCTION
Service de l'édition, Direction des expositions et de l'éducation
- Assistant Editor: Louis Gauvin
- Linguistic revision: Mireille Côté
- Translation (English version): Colleen Bilodeau
- Graphic design and computer graphics: Bleu Outremer
- Digitalization and prepress: Lacerte Communications
- Printing: K2 Impressions

ITINERARY
- Musée national des beaux-arts du Québec, Québec City
  November 24, 2005, to April 9, 2006
- Art Gallery of Windsor (Ontario)
  June 17 to September 3, 2006
- The Robert McLaughlin Gallery, Oshawa (Ontario)
  September 15 to November 5, 2006
- McCord Museum of Canadian History, Montréal (Québec)
  December 1, 2006, to April 1, 2007
- Agnes Etherington Art Centre, Kingston (Ontario)
  April 22 to July 2, 2007
- Art Gallery of Hamilton (Ontario)
  October 4, 2007, to January 1, 2008
- The Beaverbrook Art Gallery, Fredericton (New Brunswick)
  January 19 to March 30, 2008

Cover page and table of contents: Details from *Still Life with Apples and Grapes*,
1869 (cat. 39) and from *Self Portrait*, 1882 (cat. 44)

ISBN 2-551-22821-2
Legal deposit – Bibliothèque nationale du Québec, 2006
National Library of Canada, 2006
© Musée national des beaux-arts du Québec
Printed in Québec City, Canada

The Musée national des beaux-arts du Québec is a government corporation
funded by the ministère de la Culture et des Communications du Québec.

The exhibition received financial support under Heritage Canada's Museums
Assistance Program.

ABBREVIATIONS

AHGQ Archives de l'Hôpital Général de Québec
AMUQ Archives du Monastère des Ursulines de Québec
ANQQ Archives nationales du Québec, Québec City
IBCQ Inventaire des biens culturels du Québec
MACM Musée d'art contemporain de Montréal
MAFQ Musée de l'Amérique française, Québec City
MAHDQ Musée des Augustines de l'Hôtel-Dieu de Québec
MAHGQ Musée des Augustines de l'Hôpital Général de Québec
MMFA The Montreal Museum of Fine Arts
MNBAQ Musée national des beaux-arts du Québec, Québec City
NGC National Gallery of Canada, Ottawa
PA Parish archives

Table of Contents

Lenders

Private collections, Montréal and Toronto
Art Gallery of Hamilton
Art Gallery of Ontario, Toronto
Art Gallery of Windsor
Bibliothèque de l'Université Laval, Québec City
L'Archidiocèse d'Ottawa / The Archdiocese of Ottawa
McCord Museum of Canadian History, Montréal
Musée d'art contemporain de Montréal, Lavalin Collection
Musée de la civilisation, Séminaire de Québec Collection
Musée des Augustines de l'Hôpital Général de Québec
Musée national des beaux-arts du Québec, Québec City
National Gallery of Canada, Ottawa
Power Corporation du Canada / Power Corporation of Canada, Montréal
The Montreal Museum of Fine Arts

Acknowledgements

Numerous in-house and external collaborators helped in preparing the *Antoine Plamondon (1804-1895). Milestones of an Artistic Journey* exhibition and the catalogue that accompanies it. Sincere thanks to all, whatever the phase of their involvement, notably:

Sister Rita Caron, a.m.j., Janet M. Brooke, Arlene Gehmacher, Sonia Mimeault and Beverly Schaeffer; Monseignor Marcel Gervais, Father Armand Gagné, René Chartrand, Jules Dagenais, Paul-Guy Desmarais, Jacques Des Rochers, Charles C. Hill, Serge Joyal, Paul Maréchal, Rémi Morissette, Dennis Reid, Louis R. Richer and Fred Schaeffer, as well as the restorers from the painting workshop of the Centre de conservation du Québec. At the Musée national des beaux-arts du Québec there were Louise Dubois, Line Ouellet, Catherine Perron, Phyllis Smith and Nathalie Thibault; Denis Allison, Claude Belleau, Claude Bilodeau, Denis Castonguay, Daniel Drouin and in particular, Yves Lacasse, who, some time ago, compiled a wealth of documentary material about the artist. His comments on the catalogue manuscript proved invaluable.

J.R.P. and M.B.

Rediscovering Antoine Plamondon

I n 1934, a year after the opening of what was then called the Musée de la Province de Québec, Premier Louis-Alexandre Taschereau (1867-1952) gave the institution three oil paintings on canvas by Antoine Plamondon, including portraits of Amable Dionne and his wife (cat. 5 and 6). Today, the Musée national des beaux-arts du Québec collection has 42 works definitively attributed to the artist. We chose 23 to form the core of the *Antoine Plamondon (1804-1895). Milestones of an Artistic Journey* exhibition. This event, which is a first, enables us to highlight a portion of our museum heritage, while doing some timely catching up in the wake of the 200th anniversary of the birth of the artist. We were delighted that some dozen Canadian institutions, as well as collectors from Montréal and Toronto, decided to be part of the exhibition. The result is an exhibition that aptly reflects the main facets of Plamondon's body of work. Heartfelt thanks to all of them, particularly the Art Gallery of Ontario, in Toronto, which loaned us an essential work, *The Pigeon Hunt* (cat. 30), despite the moratorium in effect while expansion work on its museum is underway.

These days, organizing an exhibition dedicated to Early Québec Painting is a rare event indeed. It comes as no surprise, then, that six museums in Québec, Ontario, and the Maritimes were interested in hosting it. Thanks to funding from Heritage Canada, the exhibition will go on tour until March 2008 and be shown in Windsor, Oshawa, Montréal, Kingston, Hamilton and Fredericton. In these places, as in Québec City, visitors will be able to see for themselves, and therefore realize, that today's art has a past whose forms and colours can be appreciated provided we know how to put them in context and measure their originality by looking beyond borrowings and derivations. What's more, at every stop, the exhibition will be different, because the idea is to have each host museum add its own Plamondon works to the core exhibition.

Even for people familiar with our Early Art, there are still surprises in store— first-time juxtapositions and the presence of never-before-seen works and several recently restored paintings, including a large *Saint Francis Xavier Preaching in India*. And here, allow me to acknowledge the outstanding contribution of Claude Belleau, who spearheaded an ambitious project with his colleagues from the Centre de conservation du Québec to restore a dozen paintings from the Musée national des beaux-arts du Québec collection. Mr. Belleau also made sure that a number of paintings were given the frames they deserve.

In preparing the exhibition, we were able to draw on our very rich body of Plamondon documents and to separate the grain from the chaff, that is, the numerous works on paper that have, until now, been attributed to the artist. On this score, I would like to salute the enthusiasm and determination of Mario Béland, our Curator of Early Québec Art, 1850 to 1900, who was one of my first students at Université Laval. I truly enjoyed collaborating with him as we polished and improved each other's work.

For a museum director, there is always a certain pleasure—laced with nostalgia—in going back over terrain already traveled, and, when working on a project, rediscovering the world of research, old paintings, first-hand documents, old newspapers, and who knows what else that resurfaces. When pulling together the thread of the career of a painter as colourful as Plamondon, there is never a dull moment, especially given that this some-times excessive artist lived to a ripe old age and wore a number of hats at various stages in his life—teacher, farmer, polemicist, musician and mayor of a village in the Portneuf region!

In closing, I would like to thank renowned songwriter Luc Plamondon, originally from Portneuf County, the fourth-generation descendant of the artist, for having accepted the honourary presidency of the *Antoine Plamondon (1804-1895). Milestones of an Artistic Journey* exhibition. Four generations apart, Antoine Plamondon and Luc Plamondon not only share a family name, but also an inexhaustible passion for music, song… and painting.

Dr. John R. Porter, CQ, FRSC
Executive Director
Musée national des beaux-arts du Québec

Saint Francis Xavier Preaching in India, before conservation treatment (cat. 7). Photo Centre de conservation du Québec, Québec City, Michel Élie.

Chronology

1804, FEBRUARY 29	Born in L'Ancienne-Lorette.
1819-1825	Apprenticed to painter Joseph Légaré. Copies religious paintings and restores canvases from the Desjardins collection.
1825	Opens a studio on rue Sainte-Hélène in Québec City and advertises in *La Gazette de Québec*. Produces paintings for the Notre-Dame de Québec, Beaumont, Bécancour and Cap-Santé churches (fig. 1).
1826, JUNE 12	Announces his imminent departure for Europe and sale of his collection of paintings (fig. 2).
1826-1830	Studies in Paris under painter Jean-Baptiste-Paulin Guérin, dit Paulin-Guérin. Copies the Old Masters at the Louvre (cat. 1).
1830, NOVEMBER 3	Settles on rue Sainte-Famille in Québec City and offers his services in *La Gazette de Québec / The Quebec Gazette* (fig. 5).
1833-1835	Teaches drawing at the Séminaire de Québec.
1833	Attempts to discredit American artist James Bowman in the newspapers. Gives drawing classes at Sainte-Anne-de-la-Pocatière college.
1834	Announces opening of his studio in the Provincial Parliament Building. François Matte and Théophile Hamel become his apprentices.
1835	Attempts to discredit British artist Henry D. Thielcke in the newspapers.
1836	Spends the summer in Montréal. He offers his services in *La Minerve*, paints the portrait of Louis-Joseph Papineau (cat. 10) and begins work on the fourteen *Stations of the Cross* at Notre-Dame church (cat. 13).
1838	Is awarded the medal of the Literary and Historical Society of Québec for *The Last of the Hurons* (cat. 16), a portrait acquired by Lord Durham. Sets up his studio at Hôtel-Dieu de Québec.
1839	Exposes his *Stations of the Cross* at the House of Assembly of Québec (fig. 7).
1840	Vital Desrochers becomes his apprentice. Directs a sacred music ensemble.
1840-1845	Teaches drawing at the Séminaire de Québec.
1841	Sets up a studio across from the Anglican Cathedral and the market. Is part of a committee to establish a Vattemare Institute in Québec City. Gives drawing lessons at Hôpital Général de Québec, where he does the portraits of three nuns (cat. 18).
1841-1842	Does portraits of six members of the Guillet dit Tourangeau and Paradis families (cat. 19 to 24).
1842	Attempts to discredit French artist Victor Ernette in the newspapers. Buys land at Pointe-aux-Trembles (Neuville).
1843 AND 1845	Is part of the annual exhibition of the Mechanics' Institute (Institut des artisans).

1845	After the fires in the house beside his studio, on rue Desjardins, and in his apartment, on rue Richelieu, he sets up his studio in the former château Saint-Louis. Puts his collection of European paintings up for sale.
1845-1846	Speaks at the Société de discussion de Québec, of which he is a member.
1846	Has a house with a huge studio constructed in Neuville.
1850	Is involved in a newspaper diatribe with sculptor Thomas Fournier on the subject of the place of the fine arts in churches. Is awarded first prize at the Québec agricultural and industrial exhibition for *The Pigeon Hunt* (cat. 30).
1851	Loses his studio at château Saint-Louis and moves to Neuville, where he hires three farm workers.
1853	Is awarded first prize at the Montréal provincial exhibition for *The Pigeon Hunt*.
1855	Is named first mayor of Neuville.
1857	Takes part in an exhibition at Bonaventure Hall in Montréal.
1860-1862	Attacks Québec artists Théophile Hamel and Antoine-Sébastien Falardeau and French artist Alexandre Legrand in the newspapers.
AROUND 1865	Siméon Alary becomes his pupil.
1866-1868	Paints five versions of *The Flutist* (cat. 34 to 37).
1868-1871	Produces five versions of *Still Life with Apples and Grapes* (cat. 38 to 40).
1870	An "epigram" in his honour is published in *Le Courrier du Canada*. Denigrates the work of Italian artist Vincenzo Pasqualoni in the newspapers.
1871	Offer published to paint portraits from photographs (fig. 14). Takes part in the Québec provincial exhibition.
1874	Severely criticizes European artist Martino in the newspapers.
1877	Takes part in the Québec provincial exhibition.
1880	Exhibits 15 paintings at the Québec Parliament. Is named founding Vice President of the Canadian Academy of Arts, later the Royal Canadian Academy of Arts (Ottawa). Presents *Still Life with Apples and Grapes* as his diploma piece.
1881-1882	Sells 18 religious paintings to the Neuville church.
1882	Paints a *Self Portrait* (cat. 44). Indicates on the painting itself that *King David*, in the Neuville church, is his "last large painting."
1885	Produces his last portraits, retires, and puts the contents of his studio up for sale (fig. 15).
1895, SEPTEMBER 4	Dies a bachelor in Neuville, and is buried in the crypt of the parish church.

Plamondon *Over Hill and Vale*

John R. Porter

In hindsight, one could say that Antoine Plamondon (1804–1895), while not an especially pleasant man, was blessed with undeniable artistic talent, something he himself never doubted over the course of a career that spanned some 65 years, from 1819 to 1885.[1]

Training in Québec City and Paris (1819-1830)

The son[2] of Pierre Plamondon (a farmer) and Marie Hamel, Antoine Plamondon was born into modest means on February 29, 1804, in L'Ancienne-Lorette, a village on the outskirts of Québec City.[3] As a young boy, Antoine was taken under the wing of his parish priest and vicar general of the Diocese of Québec City, Abbé Charles-Joseph Brassard-Deschenaux (1752–1832), who helped him complete his elementary education, then encouraged him to become a painter.[4] When he signed his apprenticeship contract with master painter Joseph Légaré (1795–1855) on March 1, 1819, Antoine was living in Québec City, where his father had recently begun working as an innkeeper in the Saint-Roch district.[5] Antoine had just turned fifteen, and was bound by his obligation towards his master until he reached the age of majority. Légaré was then a young artist with little experience. A painter and glazier by training, Légaré had taken the opportunity to teach himself the rudiments of artistic painting from the first shipment to Québec City, in 1817, of paintings from the Desjardins[6] collection, thus embarking on a more rewarding career.[7]

During the six years of his apprenticeship, Plamondon learned to paint and draw on the job, helping produce copies of religious works,[8] restore paintings from the Desjardins collection,[9] and even perform certain tasks more in keeping with his master's earlier profession.[10] In March 1825, he left Légaré to set up on his own in a studio on rue Sainte-Hélène in Québec City.[11] One year later, no doubt realizing the limits of his training (fig. 1), Plamondon expressed an interest in perfecting his skills in Europe,[12] the Desjardins collection having opened his eyes to the artistic treasures to be found there.[13]

Fig. 1
The Miracles of Saint Anne, 1825; oil on canvas, 300 x 200 cm (approx.); signed and dated lower right: Ant. Plamondon Pinxit / 1825. Side altar of Sainte-Famille church, Cap-Santé.

Antoine left Québec City in July 1826, after selling a number of his copies of religious works as well as "several original European paintings"[14] (fig. 2). He was likely accompanied by his cousin Ignace (1796–1835), eight years his elder, who was also pursuing an artistic career, and wished to continue his training in Paris.[15] Armed with letters of recommendation from Abbé Louis-Joseph Desjardins (1766–1848) to his brother Abbé Philippe-Jean-Louis Desjardins (1753–1833), vicar general at the Archdiocese of Paris, the two young men enjoyed the protection of the latter for the duration of their studies under painter Jean-Baptiste Paulin-Guérin (1783–1855),

Fig. 2
Advertisement by Plamondon, *La Gazette de Québec*, June 12, 1826, p. 2.

Fig. 3
Self Portrait, 1827; oil on canvas, 59.5 x 48.7 cm; signed and dated on the reverse side of the canvas (before rebacking): Portrait fait à Paris par A. Plamondon / le 20 mai 1827 / Ant. Plamondon / 20 mai 1827.
Musée national des beaux-arts du Québec, Québec City, gift of Mr. André Hamel (62.97).

a conscientious artist heedful of the day's values, who, in 1828, was named director of drawing and painting studies at Maison royale de Saint-Denis.[16] The Plamondon cousins were not terribly resourceful and were apparently something of a burden to their protector, who went so far as to refer to them as "babes in arms."[17] According to Bellerive, Antoine did, however, take advantage of his stay in Europe to visit the Italian cities of Rome, Florence, and Venice.[18]

Caught in the midst of the political turmoil of July 1830 that led to the fall of Charles X, a terrified Plamondon holed up in his boarding room for three days. When calm finally returned to the city, he remained traumatized by the events he had witnessed,

events that served to strengthen his monarchist convictions and his hatred of red republicans.[19] He hastened home in the fall of 1830, much relieved to be back in Québec City.[20]

The young Antoine brought back a self portrait (fig. 3), a copy of a work by Titian hanging in the Louvre (cat. 1), and a copy of two paintings by his master Guérin—a portrait of Abbé Philippe-Jean-Louis Desjardins and *The Despair of Cain* (fig. 4).[21]

Fig. 4
The Despair of Cain, after Jean-Baptiste-Paulin Guérin,
dit Paulin-Guérin, 1826-1830; oil on canvas, 64.6 x 80.8 cm;
signed and dated lower right: A. Plamondon.
Musée de la civilisation, Séminaire de Québec Collection (1991.44).

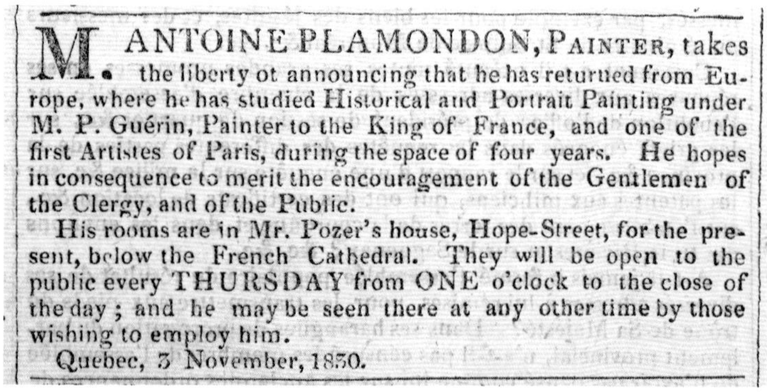

M. ANTOINE PLAMONDON, PAINTER, takes the liberty ot announcing that he has returned from Europe, where he has studied Historical and Portrait Painting under M. P. Guérin, Painter to the King of France, and one of the first Artistes of Paris, during the space of four years. He hopes in consequence to merit the encouragement of the Gentlemen of the Clergy, and of the Public.

His rooms are in Mr. Pozer's house, Hope-Street, for the present, below the French Cathedral. They will be open to the public every THURSDAY from ONE o'clock to the close of the day; and he may be seen there at any other time by those wishing to employ him.

Quebec, 3 November, 1830.

Fig. 5
Advertisement by Plamondon, *The Quebec Gazette*, November 3, 1830.

Québec City Period (1830-1850)

Plamondon informed his clientele that he was back in the capital of Lower Canada by placing an ad in English and French in the November issue of *The Quebec Gazette*[22] (fig. 5). With his natural talent, nurtured by sound European training, he was quick to capitalize on the prestige of his association with Paulin-Guérin, "Painter to the King of France,"[23] and churned out numerous copies of religious paintings[24] (cat. 7) as well as portraits of members of the French and English bourgeoisie (cat. 4 to 6), the Catholic clergy (cat. 8), and military men.[25] Plamondon's remarkable 1832 portrait of Cyprien Tanguay (cat. 2), a young Séminaire de Québec student, clearly bears the mark of the training he received at the hand of his French master.[26] During this period, he painted an unusual *Vanity* (fig. 6) for the Ursulines Sisters of Québec City[27] and also undertook a large copy of Raphael's *Transfiguration*, an "enormous task" that required him to restrict access to his studio on rue Sainte-Famille.[28] The self-important young man soon considered Québec City as his own private domain. In 1833, he gave full vent to his jealous and intolerant temperament, ridiculing in the newspapers the diorama painted by his American competitor James Bowman (1793–1842).[29] The same year, taking the stance of grand connoisseur, he lambasted the editors of the Montréal and Québec City newspapers for daring to extol the merits of a set of paintings by masters of the Italian and Flemish schools.[30]

While his arrogant remarks earned him scathing rebuffs,[31] they don't appear to have dampened his growing success or public admiration for his work, as illustrated by the glowing praise from Reverend Daniel Wilkie (1777–1851) in an address to the Literary and Historical Society of Québec in December 1833.[32] In addition to saluting Plamondon's natural talent and outstanding training, Wilkie also lauded his skill as a copyist and virtuoso portrait painter, even going so far as to qualify his likenesses of military men as "really *chef d'œuvres*" (cat. 3). Calling on his audience to encourage the artist, he deplored the fact that Plamondon was still toiling away in a mere shed, and suggested that the government provide him with a decent place to work in the newly erected House of Assembly.[33]

In April 1834, Plamondon announced with obvious delight that, thanks to the generosity of the Speaker of the House of Assembly, Louis-Joseph Papineau (1786–1871) and the Assembly Clerk, as of the following month, he would have "an apartment in the magnificent provincial parliament building in which to work on his paintings."[34] But his satisfaction was tempered by the discovery that British portrait painter Henry D. Thielcke (1787–1874) was to enjoy a similar privilege and, to make matters worse, would occupy the studio adjacent to his own.[35] The following year, Thielcke completed several religious paintings,[36] and even exhibited a painting of the *Baptism of Christ* in his studio to favourable reviews by *Le Canadien* and the *Quebec Mercury*. This was too much

SPECULUM MISERIÆ ET FRAGILITATIS HUMANÆ.

for Plamondon, who couldn't bear the thought of his studio neighbour making significant inroads in a market he considered his and his alone. Writing under the pseudonym "Des Amateurs," he immediately heaped scorn on his competitor's work, criticizing his drawing and use of colour.[37] His contemptuous comments had a disastrous effect on Thielcke's career in Quebec, forcing him to abandon any further attempts at religious painting.

By this time, Plamondon was the most sought-after artist in Lower Canada, with commissions flooding in from all sides. In 1835, he painted a portrait of Bishop Pierre-Flavien Turgeon (1787–1867), the coadjutor to the Archbishop of Québec City, Joseph Signay (1778–1850).[38] The following year, Signay in turn commissioned work from Plamondon, who magnanimously agreed to spend the summer away from Québec City in order to comply with "the repeated requests of several of Montréal's leading citizens."[39] Delighted at his arrival in Montréal, *La Minerve* hailed him as the "most talented painter in the country."[40] During his stay in Montréal, Plamondon was in

such demand that he was obliged to turn down work.[41] In addition to landing a major commission for fourteen large paintings depicting the Stations of the Cross for Notre-Dame church, he also painted numerous family portraits, including those of manufacturer Thomas B. Wragg (1799–1876) and his wife, as well as entrepreneur and industrialist John Redpath (1796–1869) and his second wife[42] (cat. 12). The great patriot Louis-Joseph Papineau, then at the peak of his political career, commissioned his own portrait and another of his wife and of his daughter Ézilda[43] (cat. 10 and 11). It was probably under the same circumstances that Papineau acquired a copy of Titian's *Young Woman at the Mirror*[44] (cat. 1), a work that Antoine undoubtedly placed in the category of "genre scenes and fantasy pictures,"[45] along with the romantic work *Lost in the Wood* that he painted the same year for Québec City lawyer Edward Burroughs[46] (cat. 9).

Fig. 6
Vanity, 1832; oil on canvas, 61.5 x 83 cm; signed and dated on the reverse side of the canvas (in ink): Ant. Plamondon / Pinxit 1832.
Musée des Ursulines de Québec.

EXHIBITION
DE LA PASSION DE N. S. JÉSUS-CHRIST
EN 14 TABLEAUX,
DE 8 PIEDS DE LARGE SUR 5 DE HAUT
PEINT PAR
ANT. PLAMONDON, ARTISTE.

LES sujets suivants sont maintenant exposés à la GARDE ROBE de la CHAMBRE d'ASSEMBLÉE pour quelques jours seulement :

I. Tableau,—Mon Père, détournez, s'il vous plaît de moi ce calice. Néanmoins que ma volonté ne se fasse point, mais la vôtre. St. Luc. ch. 22 v. 42.

II.—Quoi ! Judas, avec un baiser, vous livrez le fils de l'homme. St. Luc ch. 22 v. 48.

III.—Si j'ai bien parlé ; pourquoi me frappez-vous ? St. Jean ch. 18 v. 23.

IV.—Une servante vint à lui, qui lui dit ; vous étiez aussi avec Jésus de Nazareth. St. Mat. ch. 26 v. 69.

V.—Hérode le fit revêtir par moquerie d'une robe blanche. St. Luc ch. 23 v. 11.

VI.—Pilate fit prendre Jésus, et le fit flageller. St. Jean ch. 17 v. 1.

VII.—Puis entrelaçant des épines, ils en firent une couronne qu'ils lui mirent sur la tête ; ils lui mirent aussi un roseau à la main droite. St. Mat. ch. 27 v. 29.

VIII.—Pilate dit : Voilà que je vous l'amène dehors, afin que vous sachiez que je ne trouve en lui aucun sujet de condamnation. Jésus sortit donc, portant une couronne d'épines et un manteau de pourpre, et Pilate leur dit ; Voilà l'homme. St. Jean ch. 19 v. 4 et 5.

IX.—Pilate se lavant les mains dit : je suis net du sang de cet homme juste. St. Mat. ch. 27 v. 24.

X.—Jésus portant sa croix, alla au lieu appelé Calvaire, qui se nomme en hébreu Golgotha. St. Jean ch. 19 v. 17.

—Mais Jésus, déjà épuisé de forces et de sang, succomba bientôt sous le faix,

XI.—Est-il une douleur semblable à la mienne ? Jéré. Lam. ch. 1 v. 12.

—Ce fut à la troisième heure du jour qu'ils l'attachèrent à la croix. Ils crucifièrent avec lui deux voleurs, un à sa droite et l'autre à sa gauche, et Jésus au milieu.

XII.—Mon Père, je remets mon ame entre vos mains, et disant ces paroles, et baissant la tête il rendit l'esprit. St. Jean ch. 19 v. 30.

XIII.—Joseph (d'Arimathie) vint trouver Pilate, et obtint de lui le corps de Jésus. Il le descendit de la croix. St. Luc ch. 24 v. 52 53.

XIV. Et dernier tableau. Joseph prit le corps, et le mit dans le sépulcre qu'il avait fait tailler dans le roc. St. Mat. ch. 27 v. 59 60.
Prix d'admission, 1s. 3d.
Québec 26 Novembre 1839.

From fall 1836 to 1839, Plamondon devoted most of his energy to the fourteen large paintings commissioned by the Sulpician Joseph-Vincent Quiblier (1796–1852) (cat. 13). To complete this ambitious undertaking, he was likely assisted by two apprentices he had hired in 1834, François Matte (1809–1839) [47] and his second cousin Théophile Hamel (1817–1870).[48] In 1838, he nonetheless found time to paint a still life of grapes (cat. 14) and a remarkable portrait of Zacharie Vincent, *The Last of the Hurons* (cat. 16), that inspired François-Xavier Garneau (1809–1866) to pen one of his most famous poems.[49] Not only did the painting earn Plamondon a first-class medal in the Literary and Historical Society's annual competition, it was also acquired shortly thereafter by none other than Governor Lord Durham (1792–1840). Later the same year, Plamondon was authorized by Abbé Jérôme Demers (1774–1853) to set up shop in a more spacious studio at Hôtel-Dieu de Québec on rue du Palais,[50] where the editor of *Le Fantasque*, Napoléon Aubin (1812–1890), paid him a visit. Aubin subsequently published a long, glowing review praising Plamondon's religious copies and portraits, and the outstanding quality of the four works in his collection by European masters.[51]

In fall 1839, the artist put the finishing touches on the Stations of the Cross paintings, and they went on display at the House of Assembly antechamber from November 27 (fig. 7). The response from the public and critics alike was so overwhelmingly favourable that the exhibition was held over for an extra week, until December 17. Consequently, one can easily imagine Plamondon's bitter disappointment upon learning that his patron was obliged to refuse the paintings that had been so widely acclaimed. Despite the technical and artistic merits of the work, eight of the subjects chosen by the artist didn't correspond to any of the traditional Stations of the Cross recognized by the Church. Given the resounding success of his exhibition, Plamondon attempted to change Quiblier's mind, but his efforts were in vain, as the Sulpician could not go against the official order he had received from Rome.[52]

In 1840, Plamondon completed one of his most accomplished copies of a religious painting, *The Descent from the Cross* by Peter Paul Rubens (1577–1640), for the high altar of the Augustines' chapel at Hôtel-Dieu de Québec, to whom he wished to express his gratitude. This remarkable and virtually complete copy made from an engraving he enlarged and embellished with his own colours, is from the central panel of the Flemish master's famous triptych hanging in the Antwerp Cathedral[53] (fig. 8).

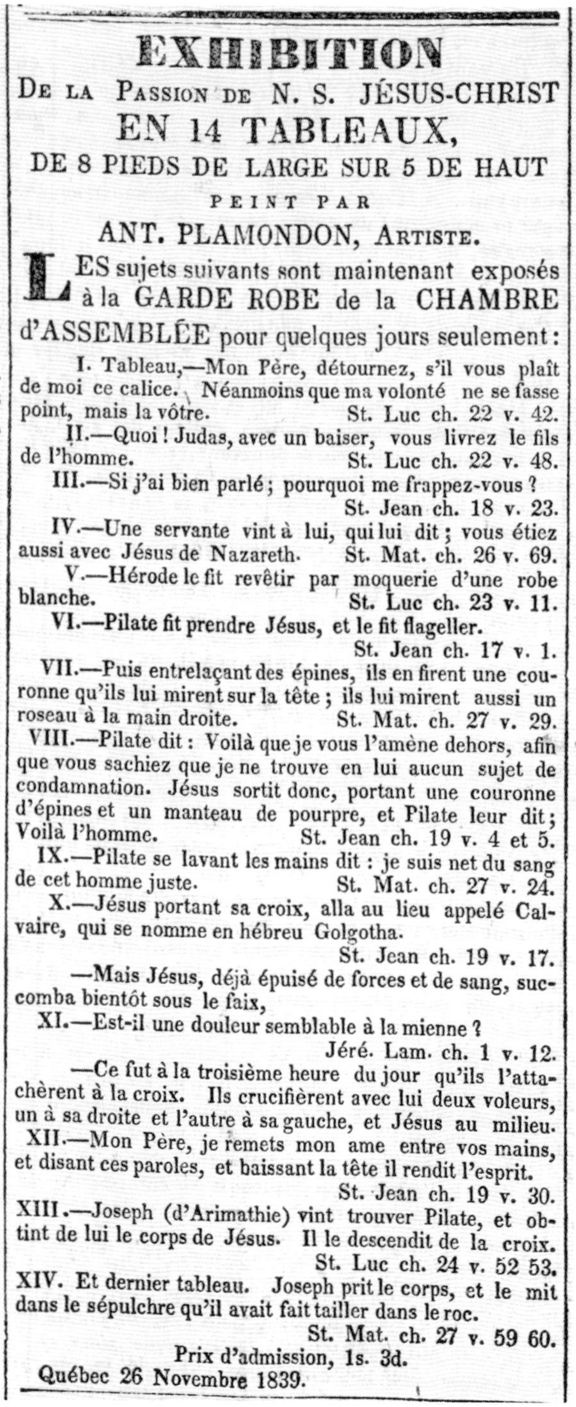

Fig. 7
Advertisement « Exhibition de la Passion de N.S. Jésus-Christ »,
Le Canadien, November 27, 1839, p. 2.

Fig. 8
The Descent from the Cross, after Peter Paul Rubens, 1840;
oil on canvas, 360 x 210 cm; signed and dated (on the first two rungs of the ladder): Plamondon / P^xit. 1840.
High altar of the church of the Augustines of the Monastère de l'Hôtel-Dieu de Québec.

In June of the same year, Plamondon found himself without an apprentice after Théophile Hamel decided to open his own studio in Québec City upon completing his training.[54] François Matte had done the same in 1838, but died prematurely the following year.[55] Plamondon began looking for a new apprentice on December 30, eventually taking on Vital Desrochers.[56] Some ten years earlier, with the backing of Abbé Jérôme Demers, Plamondon had begun giving drawing classes at Séminaire de

Québec, earning periodic praise over the years for his teaching, which continued until at least 1845.[57] In 1841, he agreed to give drawing lessons to the novices at Hôpital–Général de Québec[58] and it was during this period that he was authorized to paint his celebrated portraits entitled *Sœur Saint-Alphonse* (fig. 9), *Sœur Sainte-Anne* (cat. 18), and *Sœur Saint-Joseph*[59] (fig. 18). These outstanding works earned the artist a decidedly favourable review in *Le Canadien*, which went so far as to call Plamondon

Fig. 9
Sœur Saint-Alphonse, 1841; oil on canvas, 91.4 x 72.4 cm; signed and dated lower right (on the arm of the chair): A. Plamondon 1841.
National Gallery of Canada, Ottawa (4297).

Fig. 10
Saint Lucy Praying for the Healing of Her Mother at the Tomb of Saint Agatha, 1842; oil on canvas, 360 x 245 cm (approx.); signed and dated lower right (on the rock): A. Plamondon. / invenit. 1842.
High altar of Sainte-Luce-sur-Mer church.

the "New World's foremost colourist."[60] Offended by the pedantic and gushing tone of the article, one reader of *Le Fantasque* wrote in suggesting that the review had been concocted by the artist himself and one of his most ardent admirers, the young barrister Joseph-Édouard Cauchon (1816–1885).[61]

In 1841, Cauchon became, to all intents and purposes, Plamondon's confidant, promoter, and mentor. In addition to acquiring many of his paintings,[62] he used his position as a journalist at *Le Canadien* and later, *Le Journal de Québec*,[63] to promote his friend's work and defend his interests. One such occasion came in March 1842 when Abbé Charles Chiniquy (1809–1899)—the Beauport parish priest and temperance advocate—took possession of his portrait in oil, painted by the "brilliant brush of Mister Plamondon."[64] The following month, French painter Victor Ernette, who had earned an enviable reputation as a drawing teacher since his arrival in Quebec City,[65] denounced Plamondon's "jealous rage" and the underhandedness of "his dear Cauchon," openly accusing them of authoring an anonymous criticism of him that appeared in *Le Canadien*.[66] At that time, Plamondon completely dominated the Québec City market, monopolizing the city's clientele of wealthy bourgeois families, as demonstrated by his portraits of the Guillet dit Tourangeau and Paradis families (cat. 19 to 24), as well as his *portraits d'apparat* highlighting the social prestige of Elzéar Bédard and his wife (cat. 25 and 26).[67]

In May 1843, Cauchon penned a column in *Le Journal de Québec* overstating the merits of his protégé's "first composition" as a history painter, *Saint Lucy Praying for the Healing of Her Mother at the Tomb of Saint Agatha* (fig. 10), commissioned for the high altar of Sainte-Luce de Rimouski church.[68]

> This is the first true composition he has had the opportunity to paint. On numerous occasions, he has been required to make major changes to his compositions, and always with successful results. Very often he has had to create the colours in their entirety, as with the fourteen Stations of the Cross paintings for the church in Montréal, and who can fail to concede how well they were received, how rich the colours, how magical his touch, revealed in so many diverse and lovely forms in each painting. Many believe that colour and composition are two distinct characteristics, and that often those who are great colourists are weak at composition, and those talented at composition, weak at colour. Today, Mr. Plamondon has displayed his creation to the sceptics—those who judge a man by his past work, when he has not yet been given the opportunity to prove his great talent.

In March of the following year, Cauchon once again praised the brilliance of Plamondon, who had been commissioned by the Séminaire de Québec to paint an exact copy of *Saint Jerome Hears the Trumpet of the Last Judgement* (1717) by Pierre Dulin (1669–1748), a valuable European work that was crumbling.[69]

Cauchon was clearly not the only admirer of Plamondon's work at that time. On a one-day visit to Québec City in August 1843, Joseph-Guillaume Barthe (1816–1893), the editor of the Montréal paper *L'Aurore des Canadas*, chose to spend his entire afternoon visiting the artist's studio, which since 1841 had been in "the home of Mr. [Roger] Lelièvre (formerly a theatre) opposite the English cathedral and the market."[70] Barthe was "delighted" by everything he saw in Plamondon's showroom. After marvelling at his collection of European works, Barthe extolled the pictorial qualities of *The Little Savoyards*[71] (cat. 27), a whimsical piece inspired by an engraving of a genre painting; *Still Life with Grapes* (cat. 14), an 1838 still-life reproduction of a European canvas belonging to barrister and art collector Jean-Baptiste-Édouard Bacquet (1794–1853); *Saint Philomena*, Plamondon's most recent original work; *Saint Catherine of Sienna*, a copy of an engraving by Nicolas Bazin after the work by Domenico Feti; and *Pope Gregory XVI*, a portrait done in 1842 from a European canvas belonging to the bishop of Montréal, for which Plamondon had already received considerable acclaim[72] (fig. 11). Often accused of bias, Cauchon naturally took great delight in reprinting his Montréal colleague's article in full in *Le Journal de Québec* of September 2, 1843,[73] and several weeks later, vaunting the "exceptional" qualities of *Saint Philomena*,[74] *The Little Savoyards*[75] and the portrait of the pope.[76]

In the early 1840s, alongside his artistic endeavours, Plamondon missed no opportunity to make his presence known in Québec City, playing an active role in various social and cultural activities that served his interests or reflected his beliefs. For instance, he directed an amateur sacred music ensemble on the occasion of a solemn mass on May 20, 1840, marking the anniversary of the consecration of the archbishop of Québec City. A reporter covering the event for *Le Canadien* stated in no uncertain terms that Plamondon deserved full credit for introducing part-singing into Canadian churches.[77] In February 1841, Plamondon sat on the committee created to set up a Vattemare Institute in Québec City.[78] In April 1843, he agreed to take part in the Mechanics' Institute annual exhibition, at which Légaré and Thielcke also exhibited a few of their works.[79] The following month, he donned the cloak of moral defender, denouncing with his usual vigour the circulation of anonymous letters "containing the most loathsome slander against the honour of many respectable individuals."[80] In an entirely different matter,

Fig. 11
Pope Gregory XVI, after Pietro Gagliardi, 1842; oil on canvas, 246 x 177 cm; signed and dated lower left (on the cloth): A. Plamondon 1842.
Musée de la civilisation, Séminaire de Québec Collection (2005-5).

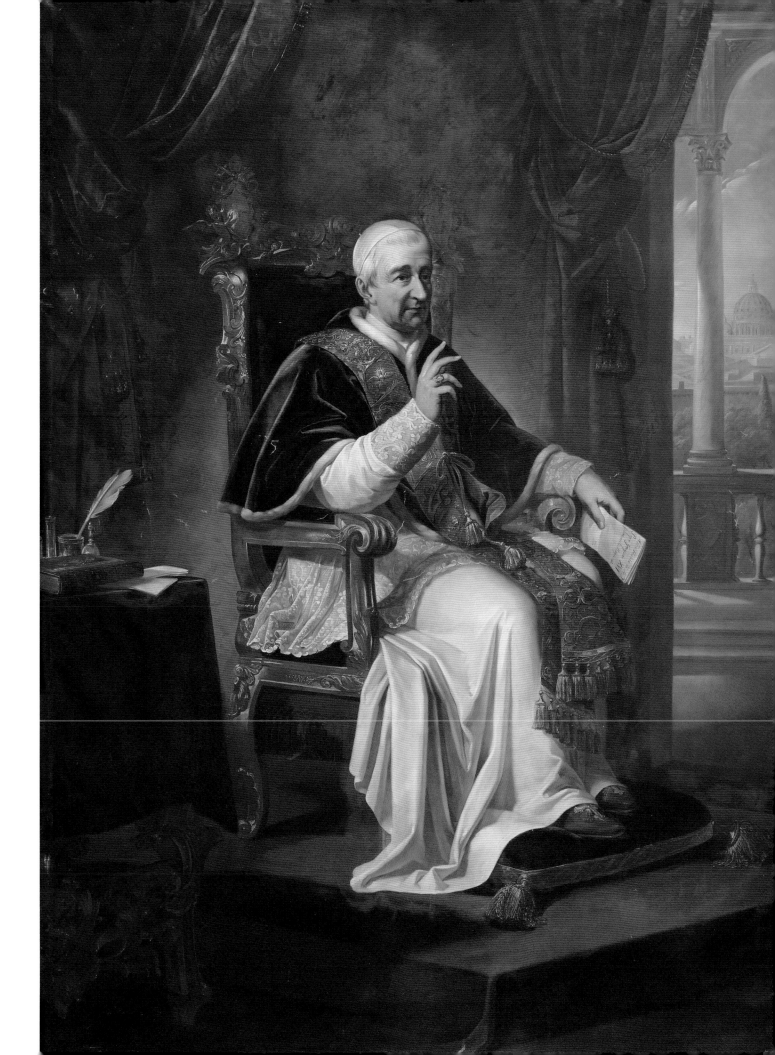

on June 10, Plamondon wrote to art collector Denis-Benjamin Viger (1774–1861) offering to sell him a painting attributed to Rubens that he had had for a number of years (Appendix, fig. 21). In September 1844, he loaned a number of his paintings to be hung in the banquet hall where the Société de discussion de Québec, a society for the intellectual advancement of all classes of society (of which he was a member), was to celebrate its first anniversary.[81] The following year he gave a three-part lecture on the origins and art of painting to the Society.[82]

The year 1845 got off to an inauspicious start for Plamondon. On January 25, fire broke out in the house adjacent to his studio. Although members of the clergy and Québec City residents rushed to remove the contents, a number of paintings were damaged during their transfer to the homes of lawyers John Urquhart Ahern and Jean-Baptiste-Édouard Bacquet. The losses exceeded the value of the artist's insurance.[83] On June 28, misfortune struck again when, exactly one month after the fire in Saint-Roch, another blaze destroyed the Saint-Jean district. Plamondon, who lived on rue Richelieu, apparently lost all his belongings in the fire, with the exception of the contents of the studio he had been occupying in the former château Saint-Louis since April.[84] Newspaper articles that appeared in August referred to his loss, noting that the artist was "obliged to part with" his precious collection of works by the European masters "in the wake of the June 28 blaze that ruined him."[85] The time was apparently not ripe for auctioning off Plamondon's six paintings.[86] Despite considerable efforts to announce the sale on September 12, it was cancelled when not enough potential buyers showed up.[87] On December 3, two months after encouraging the public to visit a diorama exhibition organized by a certain Robert Winter for the benefit of the fire victims,[88] Plamondon nearly saw the year 1845 end as it had begun, when his château Saint-Louis studio almost caught fire due to the negligence of certain members of the Oddfellows.[89]

The following year marked the return from Europe of Théophile Hamel, a highly talented portrait painter, who soon attracted a fair share of the market that had once belonged to his former master.[90] Anxious to keep up business, Plamondon shifted his focus to the production of religious works. On October 15, Cauchon made a point of noting the admirable use of colour in Plamondon's *Saint Charles Borromée* for the high altar of the Joliette church made from a "poor engraving."[91] Shortly thereafter, the artist began work on a painting of Tobias and the angel Raphael. The canvas commissioned by patron Denis-Benjamin Viger for his *censitaires* on Île Bizard was composed and sketched according to suggestions by Abbé

Jérôme Demers who, in the words of the painter, was "most demanding."[92] The painting was finally completed in October 1847. With his creditors at his heels, Plamondon requested that his sponsor pay him immediately, stressing that the work had taken him over five months to complete, and had "virtually ruined him."[93] Touched by the artist's plight, Viger not only "paid handsomely" for the large religious painting, he also purchased *The Little Savoyards*[94] (cat. 27). According to Cauchon, *Tobias and the Angel Raphael* was Plamondon's fifth or sixth original composition.[95] This appears to be the last mention of an uncopied religious painting by the artist. After a number of attempts at works of his own, it seems that Plamondon thought it more prudent and profitable to fall back on his old habits as a copyist.[96]

In fall 1848, *Le Fantasque* published a short satirical article entitled "A French-Canadian in Paris in 1830 or The pale royalist among the red republicans (historic anecdote)." Penned by Napoléon Aubin under the pseudonym Victor, the article never specifically named Plamondon, but described with acerbic wit certain episodes in the artist's life, ridiculing his failings, excessive ambition, bad temper, fearful nature, and conservative political ideas.[97] One year later, amidst debate over the question of annexation with the United States, Plamondon struck back at Aubin. Deeply stung by an article by Aubin characterizing as "rogues those who would cling to the monarchist institutions" and not wishing in any way to be mistaken for the similarly named M.A. [Marc-Aurèle] Plamondon (1823–1900), a well-known annexationist, Plamondon published a scathing attack in *Le Journal de Québec* against republicans and radicals.[98]

On February 23, 1850, the artist subjected *Le Journal de Québec* readers to a long-winded and pompous article on the nature and positive effects of good ecclesiastical paintings. To illustrate his point, he cited the masters' paintings hanging in the Séminaire de Québec chapel, remarking in passing on the beauty of one of his own works. In closing, Plamondon couldn't resist taking a potshot at church sculptors.[99] This unfortunate passage prompted an angry reply from one of his former Séminaire de Québec pupils, young ornamental carver Thomas Fournier (1825–1898).[100] In April, with the controversy between the two men barely blown over,[101] Plamondon wrote another article denouncing the mediocrity of the Stations of the Cross newly imported from France by Saint-Jean-Baptiste church in Québec City.[102]

Meanwhile, Plamondon continued producing numerous religious copies,[103] along with a number of noteworthy portraits, among them that of Vancouver bishop Modeste Demers (1809–1871)[104] (cat. 29) and Abbé Charles-François Baillargeon (1798–1870), vicar general of the Diocese of Québec City.[105] In August 1850, Plamondon and Joseph Légaré successfully experimented with pigments using a number of soil samples taken by surveyor Georges Duberger near the mouth of the Saguenay River.[106] Two months later, Plamondon took part in the Québec agricultural and industrial exhibition, where he exhibited a genre painting entitled *The Pigeon Hunt* (cat. 30). Although unfinished, this accomplished work earned him widespread public admiration and first prize in the "painting" category.[107]

Neuville Period (1851-1885)

In the spring of 1851, Plamondon learned that the government would soon need all available space in its public buildings and that he would no longer enjoy the use of his château Saint-Louis studio. Rather than despairing at the news, he quickly notified his clientele that he was relocating his studio to his property in Pointe-aux-Trembles (Neuville), a village some thirty kilometres upriver from Québec City, and that the price of his paintings would therefore be considerably reduced.[108] The artist had acquired a plot of land in Pointe-aux-Trembles in 1842.[109] Four years later he had completed a single-storey wooden house with a well-lit studio at least 18 by 30 feet with a 16 foot ceiling.[110] The 1851 census shows his property totalled 134 *arpents*—59 were wooded or fallow, 74 were pastureland for some twenty head of livestock and fields for growing grain, and the remaining *arpent* was taken up by a garden and orchard.[111] The same document shows that Plamondon boarded three young day-labourers.[112] Anxious to put the management of his farm on a firmer footing, on October 25, 1852, he hired Pierre Plamondon, a local farmer, who may or may not have been a relative.[113] The agreement was signed on the same day as his will by which he made Pierre Plamondon his executor and sole legatee, on the express condition that in the event of his death, his mother Marie Hamel and his bachelor brother Étienne, who lived with him, would be looked after by Pierre.[114]

Evidently, Plamondon's farm quickly prospered. According to the 1861 census, his land was valued at $4800 and his tilling equipment at $300. He also owned a 230-foot-long greenhouse in which he successfully grew grapes.[115] This feat was recognized in *Le Journal de Québec* in 1865[116] after the farmer/artist was cited as an example by Abbé Léon Provancher (1820–1892) in a botanical work published in 1862.[117] In the 1860s, Plamondon expanded his farm, with the 1871 census listing its size as 180 *arpents*.[118]

After settling permanently in Pointe-aux-Trembles in 1851, Plamondon earned great respect from his new fellow parishioners—simple folk impressed by his moral authority, conspicuous generosity,[119] and the prestige arising from his brilliant career as an artist. In early 1852, the farmer and history painter gave a hint of the role he planned to play from that point on in his adopted village. After severely criticizing the underhanded methods used by liberal Ulric Tessier (1817–1892) to win the provincial elections in the county of Portneuf,[120] he joined forces with the Pointe-aux-Trembles parish priest to denounce the immorality of a brochure distributed in the village in English advocating the use of contraception.[121] When the parish gained municipal status in 1855, Plamondon was named mayor by his fellow citizens.[122] That same year, he convinced his town council to pass a by-law forbidding the sale of alcoholic beverages throughout the municipality.[123]

Neither his civic responsibilities nor the running of his farm seem to have been much of an obstacle to Plamondon's artistic endeavours. During the 1850s, thirty-odd copies of religious paintings—most of them large—were sent from his vast Pointe-aux-Trembles studio to parishes across Québec.[124] As in the past, newspapers periodically made reference to his paintings, for example, in 1857, when two of his works were hung in Saint-Jean-Baptiste church in Québec City, and another at Sainte-Cécile church in Bic. This provided him with continued visibility on the arts scene, despite the fact that he was far from the capital city. On April 3, *Le Courrier du Canada* published an article by Joseph-Charles Taché (1820–1894) praising the colours of a large-scale *Assumption* copied from an engraving of the famous work by Nicolas Poussin, an artist for whom Plamondon had great admiration. However, the art critic expressed certain reservations about the addition in the upper part of the painting of a choir of six angels taken from Raphael's *Saint Cecilia*.[125] But six months later, in October, Taché had nothing but praise for the huge, fifteen-by-eleven-foot painting recently added to the north chapel of the Saint-Jean-Baptiste church, and copied "from an excellent engraving" of Raphael's famous *Transfiguration* in the Vatican. Claiming to speak on behalf of all his fellow Canadians, he warmly thanked Plamondon for completing such a brilliant "copy of the most beautiful painting ever created by the hand of man." Plamondon had begun the work in 1832 but had to set it aside until 1855.[126] In December, Plamondon again earned high praise for his large painting of *Saint Cecilia* newly hung above the high altar of the Bic church and based on a copy of the work by Raphael that had been brought over from Europe in 1830.[127]

In the early 1860s, Plamondon (fig. 12) expressed discontent on three occasions at the marked drop in demand for his work—a direct result of increasing competition from a variety of artists. In March 1860, the "history painter/farmer" lashed out at the government, blaming authorities for failing to commission a single painting marking the "sublime" history of Canada's pioneers, while agreeing to shell out large amounts of money for some thirty portraits of the speakers of the House of Assembly and the Legislative Councils—works he considered entirely devoid of interest.[128] This was a veiled attack against his former pupil Théophile Hamel, who had just completed the government contract awarded to him in 1853.[129] On September 3, 1861, Plamondon used the recent acquisition by the Québec City Sisters of Charity of a huge, twenty-seven-foot-high painting by Parisian artist Alexandre Legrand

(1822–1901) as a pretext to express his resentment with the trend to import religious paintings from Europe. After describing Legrand's *Sacred Heart* in ironic tones, he went so far as to claim that the painting lacked inspiration since "for a painter to accurately depict a sacred subject, he absolutely must have been raised in the Roman Catholic faith."[130] In August 1862, Plamondon couldn't resist commenting on the recent success of his compatriot Antoine Sébastien Falardeau (1822–1889) on the occasion of his first trip back to Canada since leaving for Italy in 1846.[131] Jealous of the warm welcome the famous copyist received from many art enthusiasts during his one-month stay in Canada,[132] Plamondon published a scathing criticism of Falardeau's works, without even bothering to mention the man's name,[133] an article that earned him a stinging rebuke from one of Falardeau's admirers.[134]

Fig. 12
Jules-Isaïe Livernois (Québec City, 1830-1865), *Antoine Plamondon*, around 1860; albuminized paper, visiting card format.
Archives nationales du Québec, Québec City.

In a tirade published on August 2, 1862, Plamondon didn't hesitate to praise the qualities of his own religious copies, declaring in the same breath that he was still receiving commissions for such paintings. In truth, his commissions were drying up, which may explain his jealous outbursts. While the 1860s were a slow period for Plamondon,[135] he did paint a number of striking secular works, among them the official portrait (1868) of his friend Cauchon, who had been recently appointed Speaker of the Senate (fig. 13). Other works from this period included five versions of *The Flutist* painted in 1866, 1867, and 1868 (cat. 34 to 37). The subject matter admirably conveyed the artist's deep love of music,[136] and the first composition of the works reflected the cropping favoured by certain photography studios at the time.[137] The model for the five paintings was Siméon Alary,[138] a 21-year-old man who, according to the 1871 census, lived under Plamondon's roof as a "painting student."[139]

It is likely that the presence of the young pupil stirred new enthusiasm in Plamondon, who began painting with renewed vigour in 1869. That year, in addition to donating a copy of Murillo's *Immaculate Conception* to the Sisters of the Good Shepherd for the high altar of their chapel in Québec City,[140] he completed two paintings for the church in Saint-Joachim, as well as copies of Raphael's *Saint Cecilia* and *Madonna Sixtine* for Saint-Jean-Baptiste church in Québec City.[141] The solemn unveiling of these last two paintings earned the artist a glowing testimonial[142] and the publication of an "epigram" in his honour in *Le Courrier du Canada*.[143]

In summer 1870, Plamondon was delighted when *Le Courrier du Canada* published a letter by French Catholic journalist Louis Veuillot (1813–1883) deploring the mediocre quality of recent works by Italian artists. Using this conservative opinion to support his argument, Plamondon criticized "certain Québec City gentlemen who, for a number of years, have been going to great lengths to convince our venerable country parish priests to have their ecclesiastical paintings done in Rome by Italians instead of here by Canadian painters." In the same breath, he dismissed the recent portrait of bishop Elzéar-Alexandre Taschereau (1820–1898), painted in Rome by Vincenzo Pasqualoni (1819–1880), as "mere daubing."[144] Driven by an astonishing creative energy, from 1870 to 1874, Plamondon completed over forty religious paintings. Two of them—*Christ on the Cross* and *Saint John the Evangelist*—were exhibited at Québec's provincial exhibition in September 1871 along with a portrait of Pius IX and two still lifes with fruit.[145] Three years

later, at Mr. Lavigne's establishment, he exhibited a painting inspired by an engraving depicting the trial of Maréchal Bazaine.[146] In 1874, he wrote a favourable review of a landscape painted by young Quebec artist Charles Huot (1855–1930), which, given his usual harsh criticism of the work of his fellow artists, raised the eyebrows of at least one columnist.[147] However, Plamondon's fiery temper boiled over again in November, when he directed a blistering attack at a set of transparencies painted two months earlier by a European artist named Martino for the celebrations marking the appointment of Bishop Taschereau to the cardinalate.[148] An angry Martino admirer responded with a harsh rebuke, accusing Plamondon of using the defense of art as a pretext to "shamelessly promote" his own paintings and to disparage an artist whose recent success in religious painting overshadowed his own.[149] Deeply offended by the remarks, Plamondon largely proved the author's point not long after by publishing a vitriolic and xenophobic criticism of Martino's recent work for the Beauport, Saint-Raymond, and Saint-Augustin churches.[150]

Despite his advancing age, Plamondon remained very active for another ten years or so. According to a short article that appeared in *Le Courrier du Canada* on August 9, 1877, he was still working four hours a day.[151] In March 1880, fifteen of his oil paintings went on display in one of the rooms at the Quebec Parliament.[152] That same year, he was named founding Vice President of the Canadian Academy of Arts, and submitted as his reception piece his *Still Life with Apples and Grapes*, having painted four analogous versions between 1868 and 1871[153] (cat. 38, 39, and 40). In 1884, Plamondon donated four paintings—a battle of lions, a still life with flowers, and two portraits of Bishop Joseph-Gauthier-Henri Smeulders (1826–1891), Canada's apostolic delegate—for the annual bazaar to raise funds for Québec City's Hôtel-Dieu du Sacré-Cœur.[154]

Three years earlier, the artist had graciously donated to the nuns of Hôtel-Dieu du Sacré-Cœur two portraits of members of the clergy copied from photographs.[155] This had become a common practice for Plamondon since March 1871, when he published an ad offering to paint portraits of various sizes from good quality photographs, so long as they were accompanied by information on complexion, eyes, hair, and beards (where applicable)[156] (fig. 14). While he was open to commissions from "anywhere in the country," his clientele by this time consisted largely of his local parishioners (cat. 43 and Appendix, fig. 25). Increasingly unsure of his own abilities, Plamondon even resorted to working from a photograph (cat. 45) to paint his self portrait in 1882 (cat. 44). Four years earlier, he had boldly ventured beyond the realm of copying to paint one of his rare imaginative works, *Revery in Venice*, a rather mediocre painting that, like many of his others, remained unsold.

From 1875 until his definitive retirement, Plamondon couldn't bring himself to give up his brushes, preferring instead to keep painting, despite the gradual loss of his abilities, the decline of his art, and the virtual absence of potential buyers for his work (cat. 42). As a result, he had no choice but to give away or sell his paintings for a pittance, his generosity being the only thing for which he could now earn credit. Plamondon not only sold 18 large religious paintings he had painted in 1881 and 1882[157] to his parish church for a small sum, he also donated a *Virgin Mary* and *Saint Joseph* to the Confrérie des Enfants de Marie and to Saint Joseph's Union in Pointe-aux-Trembles to decorate their respective banners,[158] and made a handsome contribution to his parish church in 1884 towards the purchase of a Déry organ.[159] His generosity garnered him heartfelt praise, which was naturally picked up by the Québec City newspapers.

Wishing to live out his final years in peace, in July 1883, Plamondon signed an *inter vivos* deed of gift, in which he named a Pointe-aux-Trembles farmer, Eugène Soulard, as owner of his five plots of land and all his material possessions, with the exception of his paintings, instruments, and sheet music, as well as the contents of his studio. In return, Soulard agreed to take care of his benefactor and his brother Étienne until their deaths.[160] The last known works by the artist—two portraits of prominent Pointe-aux-Trembles citizens—date from 1885. In February of the same year, Plamondon published in *Le Courrier du Canada* a notice informing the public that, due to his advanced age, he had to "lay down pencil and brush" and sell the contents of his studio, which consisted of some thirty salon paintings, of four large portfolios of drawings and of engravings of works by the old masters, as well as of numerous

BEAUX-ARTS.

AVIS. Le soussigné se charge de faire des POR-TRAITS d'après de bonnes Photographies. On recevra ces photographies sous enveloppe de lettre adressée de n'importe quelle partie du pays. On aura le soin d'indiquer dans un petit billet, la couleur des yeux, des cheveux et de la barbe, et dire aussi un peu la couleur du visage.

Le prix des portraits est comme suit : sur des toiles préparées en Angleterre.

Grand buste : toile de 4 pieds 5 pouces x 3 pieds 5 pouces,............................... $40 00
Moyen buste : toile de 3 pieds 4 pouces x 2 pieds 6 pouces,........................... 25 00
Simple buste : c'est-à-dire la tête, les épaules et la poitrine, sur toile de 2 pieds 5 pouces x 2 pieds.. .... 18 00

Si la ressemblance ne se trouve pas à la satisfaction de la personne qui la fera faire, elle ne sera pas tenue de la payer.

L'exécution des portraits sera tout ce qu'un peintre qui a plus de quarante années de pratique peut y mettre d'art.

Des portraits qui peuvent être ressemblants mais exécutés sans art, ne sont bon qu'à placer dans une cuisine, ils ne peuvent orner un salon.

ANT. PLAMONDON.
Elève de Paulin Guérin, peintre du roi Charles X, à Paris.
Pointe-aux-Trembles de Québec, comté de Portneuf, 23 mars 1871.   265-3f

volumes on art[161] (fig. 15). In the fall of the following year, the newspapers reported the death of Zacharie Vincent (1815–1886), noting that the self-taught Huron artist had studied the rudiments of painting for a time under Plamondon.[162] A man of extraordinary stamina, Plamondon lived for another ten years before passing away on September 4, 1895.[163] As a mark of the great respect he had enjoyed since settling in Pointe-aux-Trembles in 1851, he was given the honour of being buried in the crypt of the parish church.[164]

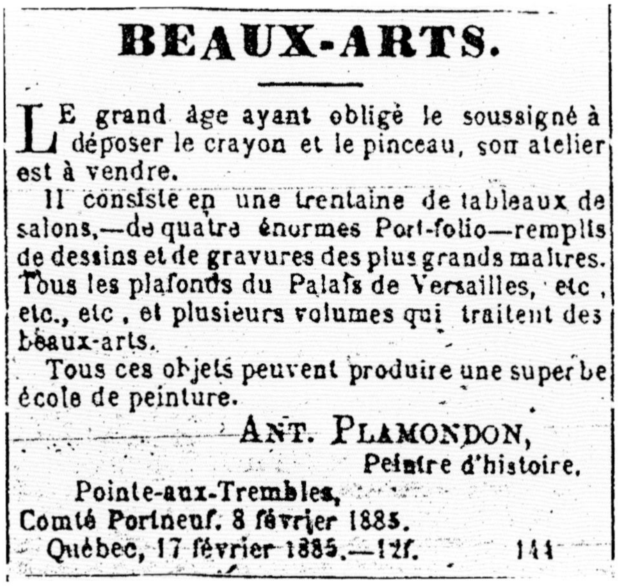

The Man and the Artist

From a physical standpoint, Plamondon had a rather disproportionately large head for his slender frame, but what stood out about him most were his expressive features, unusual ways, and odd behaviour. An unfailingly punctual man with a frugal appetite, he ate at the same time every day, and never strayed from his work habits. His taciturn nature made him intolerant of humour and levity. He was a sparing man, and couldn't abide luxury or women.[165] He was extremely conservative, not only in his political beliefs, but also in his moral and religious values. He was morbidly fearful of change and new ideologies. In spite of his perfunctory schooling, he was regarded as an educated man. While he often impressed his interlocutors with his bookish quotes, in fact his general knowledge was quite superficial, as is evident from the various newspaper articles and letters he wrote. Apart from their pretentious tone, they are dotted with truisms, frequent contradictions, and singular lapses in vocabulary and style.

Full of self-importance and jealous in the extreme, Plamondon could not bear to be contradicted and always took umbrage at the success of others. His apprentice Siméon Alary harboured unpleasant memories of the years spent with the artist in Pointe-aux-Trembles, judging by this excerpt from a letter addressed to barrister Charles Darveau in September 1917:

> What, my dear friend, can I say about my drawing and painting master Mr. Plamondon, except that he made me waste the best years of my life (my youth) with his unkept promises. He was jealous of the prizes I won at exhibitions, jealous, I should add, to the point of berating me for winning out over so many others. What I suffered during the 10 or 12 years I spent in this house, only I can say.[166]

BEAUX-ARTS.

LE grand âge ayant obligé le soussigné à déposer le crayon et le pinceau, son atelier est à vendre.

Il consiste en une trentaine de tableaux de salons,—de quatre énormes Port-folio—remplis de dessins et de gravures des plus grands maîtres. Tous les plafonds du Palais de Versailles, etc , etc., etc , et plusieurs volumes qui traitent des beaux-arts.

Tous ces objets peuvent produire une superbe école de peinture.

ANT. PLAMONDON,
Peintre d'histoire.

Pointe-aux-Trembles,
Comté Portneuf. 8 février 1885.
Québec, 17 février 1885.—12f.   141

Fig. 15
Advertisement by Plamondon, « BEAUX-ARTS », *Le Courrier du Canada*, February 18, 1885, p. 3.

His faults and shortcomings aside, Plamondon was a prolific and talented painter with undeniable artistic sensitivity, whose long career and many writings shed essential light on key aspects of the development of Canadian painting in the 19th century. With the exception of a few still lifes and genre paintings, he devoted himself primarily to portraits and religious works. In the first half of his career he was indisputably the portrait painter *par excellence* of Lower Canadian high society. His patrons—clergymen, seigneurs, politicians, merchants, and members of the liberal professions—appreciated both the accuracy of his likenesses and their classical manner. Plamondon was skilled at capturing the distinctive features and character of those who sat for him, and could paint with equal conviction works of gravity and spirituality or grace and charm. While he adhered faithfully to a number of conventions, he achieved distinction through his proven technical mastery, careful composition, harmonious use of colour, and occasionally whimsical realism in the rendering of flesh tints and textures. After 1850, he could no longer hold his own against such competitors as Théophile Hamel, and also began to suffer from the growing popularity of photography. From 1871 on, he often resorted to painting portraits from photographs, but continued to insist on the necessity of going beyond the mere likeness, adding that portraits "executed without art are good only for hanging in the kitchen." [167]

Despite claims to the contrary, Plamondon ascribed much more importance to his religious paintings than to his portraits; they accounted for more than half of his total body of work. As a history painter, he drew his inspiration from the classical tradition of Raphael, Poussin, David, and Paulin-Guérin. [168] His idea of what art is, shaped by his academic training and certain readings, was the product of pure conservatism. He believed that good ecclesiastic art should instruct and edify the faithful, while providing fitting decoration for the house of the Lord. [169]

Plamondon's copies of religious works show his marked predilection for certain great French and Italian artists of the 16th and 17th centuries, among them Raphael, Jacques Stella (whose works he sometimes confused with those of Poussin), Mignard, Titian, Domenichino, Guido Reni, and Poussin, as well as the Flemish painter Rubens. The fact remains that Plamondon's complete copies and variations of European paintings and engravings helped broaden the visual world of Canadians and acquaint them with the great art of past centuries. In his view, the copy was inseparably linked to the original—generally the object of unbounded admiration—from which it was taken. Each time he produced a good copy, Plamondon felt he had attained an ideal, and his contemporaries spontaneously associated his artistry with that of the original. He could of course display some originality in his interpretation, particularly with respect to colour, when copying from a monochrome engraving. On other occasions he expressed his own creativity by using only part of the picture being copied, or by combining elements borrowed from various iconographic sources into a new composition. [170]

Aside from the occasional stab at original paintings, Plamondon confined himself to copying throughout his career. From the 1860s, the quality of his religious canvases increasingly declined, although some of his paintings were of good quality. With increasing competition from foreign painters, he was soon overtaken by events and lost the role he had once had in the development of painting in Quebec. His deep-seated conservatism became even more extreme with the gradual loss of his abilities, overcoming any desire to explore new artistic avenues. He remained a bastion of resistance to change, a curious example of doggedness, firmly rooted in his memories. [171] It was altogether typical of him that in 1871 he still insisted on identifying himself as "the Pupil of Paulin-Guérin, Painter to Charles X in Paris..." [172]

Notes and References

1. The following text is a revised, corrected, updated, and illustrated version of a biographical entry that first appeared in 1990 in the *Dictionary of Canadian Biography*. It draws on books and articles about Antoine Plamondon published since then. See subsequent notes as well as the selective bibliography at the end of this document.

2. L'Ancienne-Lorette parish archives (hereafter PA), Civil registry, March 2, 1804 (baptism). Plamondon always believed, wrongly, that he was born in 1802 (see cat. 44). His father died on November 25, 1833, at the age of 66 (*Le Canadien*, November 27, 1833). His mother died in Pointe-aux-Trembles (Neuville) on July 18, 1865. Antoine Plamondon had two brothers: the eldest, Pierre, was apprenticed to Henry Venière (Archives nationales du Québec in Québec City [hereafter ANQQ], Notary records [hereafter NR] E. Boudreault, March 10, 1819, No. 448). The younger brother Étienne died in Neuville on June 1, 1896. Plamondon apparently also had an adoptive sister (ANQQ, Inventaire des biens culturels du Québec [hereafter IBCQ], Fonds Gérard-Morisset, Antoine Plamondon file).

3. He was related, on his mother's side, to a carpenter, Jean Levasseur dit Lavigne, who was the grandfather of the famous sculptor Noël Levasseur (1680–1740). See Hélène Lamarche, "Le peintre et l'élève modèle," *Mémoires de la Société généalogique canadienne-française*, Vol. 53, No. 3, cahier 233 (fall 2002), pp. 204–206.

4. Georges Bellerive, *Artistes-peintres canadiens-français. Les anciens*, 1ère série, Québec City, Garneau, pp. 25–26. ANQQ, IBCQ, Antoine Plamondon file (information from Lucien Lemieux, April 1, 1935). It appears that Plamondon did not undertake classical studies. Pointe-aux-Trembles PA, "Notice biographique…"

5. ANQQ, NR, Ant.-Arch. Parent, March 1, 1819, No. 916.

6. Among the most famous works of art imported in the 19th century to the British colony of Lower Canada was a group of 180 paintings that were among those seized by the revolutionary state in and around Paris from 1793 to 1795. It was Abbé Philippe-Jean-Louis Desjardins, who returned to France in 1802 after spending ten years in exile in Québec City, who acquired these paintings before sending them across the Atlantic to his brother Abbé Louis-Joseph Desjardins to be sold. Most of the paintings date from the 17th and 18th centuries, and they arrived in Québec City in two shipments, one in 1817, the other in 1820. They provided a great boost to the colony's artistic community by significantly increasing the availability of models and inspiration for local painters to copy.

7. John R. Porter, "Légaré, Joseph (1795-1855)," *Dictionary of Canadian Biography*, Vol. VIII (1851 to 1860), University of Toronto Press, 1985, pp. 494-498.

8. See *Painting in Québec 1820–1850. New Views, New Perspectives* (exhibition catalogue, ed. Mario Béland), Québec City, Musée du Québec, 1992, pp. 407–408 (note by J. Chagnon and P. Bourassa). Some of Plamondon's copies were inspired by paintings from the Desjardins collection. The first known copies by Légaré date from 1820.

9. In 1823, Plamondon worked with Louis-Hubert Triaud (1790–1836) to restore three paintings at Saint-Michel de Bellechasse church. ANQQ, IBCQ, Antoine Plamondon file.

10. Légaré and Plamondon worked on the painting and gilding of the Séminaire de Québec chapel in 1821.

11. *The Quebec Gazette*, March 31, 1825, p. 3 (advertisement dated March 26). In 1825, he completed paintings for the Beaumont, Bécancour, Notre-Dame (Québec City), and Cap-Santé churches. See *Les Chemins de la mémoire*. Vol. III: *Biens mobiliers du Québec*, Québec City, Commission des biens culturels du Québec / Les Publications du Québec, 1999, p. 254 (note by Y. Lacasse).

12. *La Bibliothèque canadienne*, June 1826, p. 36.

13. In a letter published in *Le Journal de Québec* on May 16, 1871 (p. 1), Plamondon stated that it was the Desjardins collection paintings that inspired him to go to Paris in 1826 to study painting.

14. *The Quebec Gazette*, June 12, 1826, p. 2.

15. Ignace was the son of Jacques Plamondon who, like his brother Pierre, was a farmer in L'Ancienne-Lorette. He studied under Paulin-Guérin in Paris, later prolonging his stay in Switzerland. After a seven-year voyage, he taught drawing at Chambly and Saint-Hyacinthe colleges while working as a portrait painter. He died at an early age in L'Ancienne-Lorette in June 1835. See *Painting in Québec 1820–1850, op. cit.*, pp. 440–441; *The Quebec Gazette*, November 8, 1830, p. 2; *La Minerve*, June 10, 1833, pp. 1–2; *Le Canadien*, June 19, 1835, p. 2.

16. When François-Xavier Garneau visited Guérin's studio, the artist "spoke to him with interest about his pupil, but he had made him too perfect a painter for Canada." F.-X. Garneau, *Voyages*, Québec, 1881, pp. 107–108 [1831–32–33]. Pointe-aux-Trembles PA, letter from Siméon Alary to Charles Darveau around 1915 in response to a letter Darveau sent him (November 18, 1915). Bellerive, *op. cit.*, p. 26. About Paulin-Guérin, see Jane Turner (ed.), *The Dictionary of Art*, New York, Grove, 1996, Vol. 13, pp. 790–791 (note by Jean-Roger Soubiran); Claire Constans, *Musée national du château de Versailles. Catalogue des Peintures*, Paris, Éditions de la Réunion des musées nationaux, 1980, pp. 68–69; *Le Musée a cent ans*, catalogue for an exhibition that ran at Musée de Toulon from December 21, 1988, to June 6, 1989, Vol. I, pp. 243–244.

17. "Speaking of the Plamondons—for the love of God, don't send me any more babes in arms." Monastère des Ursulines de Québec archives (hereafter AMUQ), letter from Philippe-Jean-Louis Desjardins to Louis-Joseph Desjardins and Mère Saint-Henry, October 22, 1827.

18. Bellerive, *op. cit.*, p. 26.

19. *Le Fantasque*, October 14, 1848, pp. 126–128; Bellerive, *op. cit.*, pp. 26–27.

20. The November 8, 1830, issue (p. 2) of *La Minerve* notes that he stopped in Montréal on his way home to Québec City.

21. See Mario Béland, "Antoine Plamondon au Louvre," *Cap-aux-Diamants*, No. 46 (Summer 1996), p. 58; *Painting in Québec 1820–1850, op. cit.*, pp. 411–412 (note by J.R. Porter).

22. He set up his temporary studio at the home of Mr. Pozer on rue Sainte-Famille near Notre-Dame cathedral.

23. "Painter to the King of France"—Paulin-Guérin was rather the painter of the King *of* France, as he was commissioned to paint the monarch's portrait in 1827. It was a conventional style work that hangs today in Musée de Toulon. See *Le Musée a cent ans, op. cit.*, p. 243. Despite the overthrow of Charles X in 1830, Plamondon continued to hitch his artistic prestige to the French monarchy for the duration of his career (see fig. 14). *The Quebec Gazette / La Gazette de Québec*, November 8, 1830.

24. In the early 1830s, he worked for the parishes of Saint-Roch de Québec, Saint-Jean-Baptiste des Écureuils, Baie Saint-Paul, and Saint-Augustin. See *Painting in Québec 1820–1850, op. cit.*, pp. 416–417 (note by P. Bourassa).

25. See *Painting in Québec 1820–1850, op. cit.*, p. 413 (note by P. Bourassa) and pp. 418–419 (note by M. Béland).

26. *Painting in Québec 1820–1850, op. cit.*, pp. 414–415 (note by J.R. Porter); Didier Prioul, "Livrimages. Pouvoir, plaisir et persuasion de la lecture," in *"Tous ces livres sont à toi !" De l'œuvre des bons livres à la Grande Bibliothèque (1844–2005).* Inaugural exhibition catalogue for the Grande Bibliothèque, Bibliothèque nationale du Québec, Québec City and Montréal, Les Presses de l'Université Laval and BNQ, 2005, p. 116.

27. This strange and macabre painting evoking the fleetingness of time, worldly illusions, the precarity of life, and the inevitable finality of all human beings surely had an impact on the nuns. Its Latin inscription identifies the prone skeleton as "the mirror of misery and human fragility." John R. Porter, "Le chrétien devant la mort," *Le Grand Héritage : l'Église catholique et les arts au Québec* (exhibition catalogue), Québec City, Musée du Québec, 1984, p. 312.

28. *The Quebec Gazette*, October 12, 1832, p. 2; *Le Canadien*, October 17, 1832, p. 2.

29. *Le Canadien*, July 24, 1833, p. 2.

30. *Le Canadien*, September 27, 1833, p. 2.

31. *The Quebec Mercury*, July 27, 1833, p. 3; *Le Canadien*, September 27, 1833, p. 3.

32. *The Quebec Gazette*, December 13, 1833, p. 2; *The Quebec Mercury*, December 19, 1833, p. 1; *The Montreal Gazette*, December 31, 1833, pp. 1–2.

33. Wilkie's exact words were "a mere hangar."

34. *Le Canadien*, April 21, 1834, p. 2. His studio was on the second floor in room 23.

35. *The Montreal Gazette*, May 24, 1834, p. 2. Thielcke's studio was in room 21.

36. In February 1835, he put a *Crucifixion* and a *Holy Family* of his own composition up for sale. *Le Canadien*, February 4, 1835, p. 4. John R. Porter, "Antoine Plamondon (1804–1895) et le tableau religieux…," in *Journal of Canadian Art History*, Vol. VIII, No. 1 (1984), pp. 17–18.

37. *Le Canadien*, September 2, 1835.

38. *Le Canadien*, June 19, 1835, p. 2. *Painting in Québec 1820–1850, op. cit.*, p. 424 (note by J.R. Porter).

39. Plamondon left Québec City on June 17 (*Le Canadien*, June 10 and 17, 1836) and returned in early October (*La Minerve*, September 29, 1836, and *Le Canadien*, October 10, 1836).

40. *La Minerve*, June 27, 1836, p. 2.

41. *La Minerve*, September 29, 1836, p. 3.

42. Yves Lacasse, *Antoine Plamondon (1804–1895). The Way of the Cross of the Church of Notre-Dame de Montréal* (exhibition catalogue), The Montreal Museum of Fine Arts, 1984, pp. 28-30. *Le Canadien*, October 10, 1836, p. 2. *Painting in Québec 1820–1850, op. cit.*, pp. 426–427 (note by P. Bourassa).

43. *Painting in Québec 1820–1850, op. cit.*, pp. 420–423 (note by J.R. Porter).

44. ANQQ, Fonds Papineau-Bourassa, letter from John Burroughs to Amédée Papineau, August 1891.

45. *La Minerve*, September 29, 1836, p. 3.

46. *Painting in Québec 1820–1850, op. cit.*, p. 425 (note by M. Béland).

47. ANQQ, NR, Ant.-Arch. Parent, March 28, 1834.

48. ANQQ, NR, Ant.-Arch. Parent, July 5, 1834. About the family ties between Plamondon and Hamel, see Lamarche, *op. cit.*, pp. 204–206.

49. *Painting in Québec 1820–1850, op. cit.*, pp. 352-353 and 428 (notes by L. Lacroix) and 429-431 (note by Y. Lacasse). See also François-Marc Gagnon, "Le dernier des Hurons. L'image de l'autre comme image de soi," in *Où va l'histoire de l'art contemporain*, eds. Laurence Bertrand Dorléac *et al.*, Paris, École nationale supérieure des Beaux-Arts, 1997, pp. 177–189.

50. *Le Canadien*, July 10, 1838, p. 2; *Le Fantasque*, July 21, 1838; *The Quebec Mercury*, July 25, 1838, p. 1. Hôtel-Dieu de Québec archives, "Notes et mémoires des anciennes mères," ar. 5, no. 11, f. 8 (1838).

51. *Le Fantasque*, July 28, 1838, pp. 136–138.

52. Lacasse, *op. cit.*, pp. 28–40, and *Painting in Québec 1820–1850, op. cit.*, pp. 431-432 (note by Y. Lacasse). Plamondon replied on December 16, 1839, to the letter Quiblier had sent him nine days earlier.

53. See John R. Porter and Mario Béland, "Échos de l'œuvre du maître. L'influence de Rubens sur l'art au Québec," in *Rubens et l'art de la gravure*, a book accompanying the exhibition *Copyright Rubens: The Art of a Great Image-Maker* presented at Koninklijk Museum Voor Schone Kunsten Antwerpen (Royal Museum of Fine Arts, Antwerp) from June 12 to September 12, 2004, and at Musée national des beaux-arts du Québec (Québec City) from October 14, 2004, to January 9, 2005, Gand and Amsterdam, Ludion, 2004, pp. 156-171.

54. *Le Canadien*, June 24, 1840, p. 2.

55. AMUQ, letter from Louis-Joseph Desjardins to Mère Saint-Henry, April 12, 1838.

56. *Le Canadien*, December 30, 1840, p. 2; *La Minerve*, August 14, 1845, p. 2. About Desrochers, see *Painting in Québec 1820–1850, op. cit.*, p. 241 (biographical note by Denis Castonguay).

57. *Les Mélanges religieux*, 1841, p. 141; *Le Journal de Québec*, August 3, 1844, p. 2; *Le Canadien*, October 11, 1847, p. 2; Bellerive, *op. cit.*, p. 27. Plamondon also taught courses at Sainte-Anne-de-la-Pocatière college in 1833, as noted in this article that appeared in the August 26 issue of *La Minerve* (p. 3): "Mr. Plamondon, drawing teacher at Collège Ste-Anne, is giving free lessons to clergyman Mr. Gauthier, a professor at the college, who will continue teaching the course after the holidays."

58. Plamondon gave 34 drawing lessons, which didn't entirely satisfy the nuns at Hôpital-Général. Hôpital-Général de Québec archives (hereafter AHGQ), "Journal du noviciat," Vol. I, July 1841.

59. John R. Porter, *Antoine Plamondon: Sister Saint-Alphonse, passim*. See also *Painting in Québec 1820-1850, op. cit.*, pp. 433-435 (note by J.R. Porter). See also Laurier Lacroix, "Lire au féminin : les portraits de religieuses d'Antoine Plamondon," *Portraits des arts, des lettres et de l'éloquence au Québec (1760-1840)*, eds. Bernard Andrès and Marc-André Bernier, Québec, Les Presses de l'Université Laval, 2002, pp. 59–71.

60. *Le Canadien*, August 20, 1841, p. 2.

61. *Le Fantasque*, August 23, 1841, pp. 437-439.

62. Pointe-aux-Trembles PA, letter to Hormidas Magnan dated November 15, 1922. "The late Honourable Joseph Cauchon, former lieutenant governor of Manitoba, had in his possession a number of fairly well-renowned paintings by Plamondon. They say that he turned down a high price from certain art connoisseurs for these works. Among the paintings were…"

63. Starting in December 1842. See *Le Journal de Québec* of December 24, 1842, p. 1.

64. *Le Canadien*, March 30, 1842, p. 2. The article in *Le Canadien* prompted another response in *Le Fantasque* (April 7, 1842, p. 4).

65. In February 1842, he replaced Plamondon as drawing instructor at Hôpital Général de Québec, where his teaching was much appreciated. AHGQ, "Journal des novices," February 1842.

66. *Le Fantasque*, April 7, 1842, p. 4.

67. *Painting in Québec 1820–1850, op. cit.*, pp. 39–40 (essay by P. Bourassa) and 436–437 (note by P. Bourassa).

68. *Le Journal de Québec*, May 16, 1843, p. 1. See also Porter, "Antoine Plamondon (1804–1895) et le tableau religieux…," *op. cit.*, pp. 16–17.

69. *Le Journal de Québec*, March 21, 1844, p. 2.

70. *Le Canadien*, June 2, 1841, p. 2.

71. *Painting in Québec 1820–1850, op. cit.* pp. 438–439 (note by Y. Lacasse).

72. *L'Aurore des Canadas*, August 24, 1843, p. 2. The copy of the portrait of Pope Gregory XVI painted by Plamondon and exhibited in 1842 and 1843 caused quite a stir in the press, reflecting the appreciation of art connoisseurs and the general public alike. See *L'Aurore des Canadas*, November 24, 1842 (p. 2), December 22, 1842 (pp. 2–3), December 24, 1842 (p. 2); *L'Encyclopédie canadienne*, December 1842 (p. 399); *Le Canadien*, January 2, 1843 (p. 3), March 8, 1843 (p. 3), October 11, 1843 (p. 2); *La Minerve*, December 22, 1842 (p. 2), October 23, 1843 (p. 3); *Le Journal du Canada*, September 12, 1843; *Le Journal de Québec*, December 24, 1842 (p. 1), January 3, 1843 (p. 1 and 4), January 7, 1843 (p. 4), March 7, 1843 (p. 1), September 12, 1843, October 3, 1843; *The Quebec Mercury*, January 10, 1843.

73. *Le Journal de Québec*, September 2, 1843. p. 3.

74. *Le Journal de Québec*, September 27, 1843, p. 2.

75. *Le Journal de Québec*, October 3, 1843, pp. 2–3. See note 94.

76. *Le Journal de Québec*, October 7, 1843 (p. 2) and October 19, 1843 (p. 3).

77. *Le Canadien*, May 20, 1840, p. 3.

78. *Le Canadien*, February 26, 1841, p. 2. About the Vattemare Institute, see John R. Porter, "Un projet de musée national à Québec à l'époque de Joseph Légaré (1833–1853)," *Revue d'histoire de l'Amérique française*, Vol. 31, No. 1 (June 1977), pp. 77–78.

79. *Le Fantasque*, April 22, 1843, p. 2; *Le Canadien*, April 24, 1843, p. 3. Plamondon was slated to attend the Mechanics' Institute annual exhibition again in May 1845. *The Quebec Mercury*, May 6, 1845, p. 2.

80. *Le Journal de Québec*, May 20, 1843, p. 1.

81. *Le Journal de Québec*, September 26, 1844, p. 2.

82. *Le Journal de Québec*, January 7, 1845 (p. 2), January 16, 1845 (p. 2), and February 6, 1845 (p. 2).

83. See *Le Canadien*, January 27, 1845, pp. 2–3; *Le Journal de Québec*, January 28, 1845, pp. 2–3.

84. Plamondon lived in a house at 90 rue Richelieu belonging to Charles Marois. The Québec City assessment and tax roll for 1845 notes that the house was destroyed by fire. *Le Castor*, April 17, 1845, p. 3; *Le Journal de Québec*, April 17, 1845, p. 3; *Le Canadien*, April 21, 1845, p. 3.

85. *Le Canadien*, August 18, 1845, p. 2. See also *Le Journal de Québec*, August 23, 1845, p. 2; *L'Aurore des Canadas*, August 28, 1845, p. 2.

86. Plamondon's paintings included works by Van Ostade, Murillo, Rubens, Poussin, Peeter Tays, and Sneyder. *Idem.* Two years earlier, the artist attempted in vain to sell his "Rubens"—a 4 foot nine inch by 7 foot 6 inch *Beheading of St. John the Baptist*—to art collector and politician Denis-Benjamin Viger. MNBAQ Archives, letter from Antoine Plamondon to Denis-Benjamin Viger, June 10, 1843 (Appendix, fig. 21).

87. *Le Canadien*, September 15, 1845, p. 2; *Le Journal de Québec*, September 16, 1845, p. 2.

88. *Le Canadien*, October 6, 1845, p. 2; *L'Aurore des Canadas*, October 11, 1845, p. 2.

89. *Le Journal de Québec*, December 4, 1845, p. 2; *La Gazette de Québec*, December 5, 1845.

90. *Le Journal de Québec*, August 11, 1846, p. 2.

91. *Le Journal de Québec*, October 15, 1846, p. 2.

92. Private collection (Montréal), letter from Antoine Plamondon to Denis-Benjamin Viger, November 27, 1846.

93. McCord Museum of Canadian History Archives (Montréal), Antoine Plamondon file, letter from Antoine Plamondon to Denis-Benjamin Viger, October 28, 1847.

94. *Le Journal de Québec*, November 16, 1847, p. 2; *Le Canadien*, November 19, 1847, p. 2; *L'Aurore des Canadas*, November 23, 1847, p. 2.

95. *Le Journal de Québec*, October 14, 1847, p. 2. Like Cauchon, Napoléon Aubin wrote a long article praising the artist's work. *Le Canadien*, October 15, 1847, p. 2.

96. Porter, "Antoine Plamondon (1804–1895) et le tableau religieux…," *op. cit.*, p. 21.

97. "Un Canadien-français à Paris en 1830 ou Le Royaliste blême chez les républicains rouges (anecdote historique)," *Le Fantasque*, October 14, 1848, pp. 126–128.

98. *Le Journal de Québec*, November 3, 1849.

99. *Le Journal de Québec*, February 23, 1850, pp. 2–3.

100. *Le Journal de Québec*, March 7, 1850, p. 1. About Thomas Fournier, see *Le Canadien*, October 11, 1847, p. 2; *Le Journal de Québec*, October 12, 1847, p. 21; John R. Porter and Jean Bélisle, *La sculpture ancienne au Québec*, Montréal, Éditions de l'Homme, 1986, pp. 476–481. Ironically, it was Fournier who, in 1857, was asked to frame Plamondon's copy of the famous portrait of Pope Gregory XVI!

101. *Le Journal de Québec*, 4 (p. 2) and 11 (p. 2) April 1850.

102. *Le Journal de Québec*, April 13, 1850, p. 2.

103. See *L'Ami de la religion et de la patrie*, December 13, 1848, p. 2; *Le Journal de Québec*, June 23, 1849 (p. 2), March 12, 1850 (p. 2), and March 29, 1851 (p. 2); *L'Abeille*, June 28, 1850, p. 3.

104. *L'Ami de la religion et de la patrie*, November 10, 1848, p. 773; *La Minerve*, November 13, 1848.

105. *Le Journal de Québec*, May 25, 1850, p. 2; *Le Canadien*, May 27, 1850, p. 2. This portrait was lithographed in New York City from Plamondon's drawing. *Le Canadien*, November 18, 1850, p. 2; *Le Journal de Québec*, November 19, 1850, p. 2.

106. *Le Canadien*, August 19, 1850, p. 2; *Le Journal de Québec*, August 20, 1850, p. 2.

107. *Le Journal de Québec*, October 12, 1850, p. 2; *Le Canadien*, October 18, 1850, p. 2. This painting was displayed again in Montréal in 1853, where it earned the artist another award. See *Le Journal de Québec*, October 6, 1853, p. 2. *Painting in Québec 1820–1850, op. cit.*, pp. 570–573 (note by J.R. Porter).

108. *Le Canadien*, June 2, 1851, p. 3; *Le Journal de Québec*, June 3, 1851, p. 2. Cauchon took the opportunity to express his distress at his friend being "forced to abandon the city for a remote corner of the back and beyond." *Le Journal de Québec*, June 5, 1851, p. 2.

109. ANQQ, NR, F.-X.Larue, July 11, 1842. See also ANQQ, NR, P.H. Faucher, 29 (No. 194 and 195) and 30 (No. 196) July 1842, and February 16, 1843 (No. 210).

110. ANQQ, NR, J. Petitclerc, Markets at December 16, 1845 (No. 3392), January 13 (No. 3428), and March 31 (No. 3582), 1846. See also Yves Laframboise *et al.*, *Neuville architecture traditionnelle*, Québec City, Ministère des Affaires culturelles, 1976 (Les cahiers du patrimoine, 3), pp. 211–217 and 275–282.

111. ANQQ, 1851 Census, Pointe-aux-Trembles (Portneuf), p. 93.

112. They were aged 15, 19, and 22. *Idem*, p. 9.

113. ANQQ, NR, P.H. Faucher, Agreement dated October 25, 1852 (No. 509).

114. ANQQ, NR, P.H. Faucher, Will dated October 25, 1852 (No. 510). The 1861 census confirms that the artist's mother (age 86) and brother (age 50) resided with him in Pointe-aux-Trembles.

115. ANQQ. 1861 Census, Pointe-aux-Trembles.

116. *Le Journal de Québec*, October 4, 1865, p. 2.

117. Léon Provancher, *Le verger, le potager et le parterre dans la province de Québec; ou Culture raisonnée des fruits, légumes et fleurs du Québec*, Québec City, Darveau, 1874, pp. 140–141. We consulted the third edition of this work, which was originally published in 1862 under the name *Le verger canadien*. See also Bellerive, *op. cit*, p. 36.

118. ANQQ, 1871 Census, Pointe-aux-Trembles (Portneuf).

119. In 1854, he apparently donated a large painting of the Immaculate Conception to the Pointe-aux-Trembles parish on the occasion of the festivities surrounding the proclamation of the doctrine. Pointe-aux-Trembles PA, "Notice biographique…" See also *L'Électeur*, March 29, 1881, pp. 1–2.

120. *Le Canadien*, January 14, 1852, p. 2

121. *Le Canadien*, February 25, 1852, p. 2.

122. Bellerive, *op. cit.*, p. 35.

123. *Le Journal de Québec*, December 22, 1855, p. 2.

124. Certain parishes commissioned several works each, among them Saint-Jean-Baptiste in Québec City, Saint-Anselme, Saint-Charles de Bellechasse, Neuville, and Saint-François de l'île d'Orléans. Outside the Greater Québec City area, his customers included the parishes of Saint-Simon in Rimouski, Sainte-Philomène in Châteauguay, Sainte-Cécile in Bic, and Sainte-Anne in Yamachiche.

125. *Le Courrier du Canada*, April 3, 1857, p. 1.

126. *Le Courrier du Canada*, October 2, 1857.

127. *Le Courrier du Canada*, December 11, 1857. See Denis Grenier, "La descendance québécoise de la *Sainte Cécile* de Raphaël," *Journal of Canadian Art History*, Vol. XII, No. 2 (1989), pp. 115–138.

128. *Le Courrier du Canada*, March 21, 1860.

129. See Raymond Vézina, *Théophile Hamel. Peintre national (1817–1870)*, Montréal, Éditions Élysée, 1975, Vol. 1, p. 104; *Le Canadien*, August 13, 1862, p. 2.

130. *Le Journal de Québec*, September 3, 1861 (p. 2) and August 2, 1862 (p. 2).

131. See Émile Falardeau, *Un maître de la peinture. Antoine-Sébastien Falardeau*, Montréal, Éditions Albert Lévesque, 1936, pp. 103–120; Virginia Nixon, "Antoine-Sébastien Falardeau (1822–1889) and The Old Master Copy in the Nineteenth Century," Master's thesis submitted to Concordia University (Montréal) in September 1988.

132. He was especially angered by an article signed "C.D." that appeared in *Le Journal de Québec* on July 22, 1862.

133. *Le Journal de Québec*, August 2, 1862, p. 2.

134. *Le Canadien*, August 13, 1862, p. 2.

135. We identified only a dozen religious paintings during the 1860s.

136. See Bellerive, *op. cit.*, p. 36.

137. For example, the composition of a photograph of Bishop E.-A. Taschereau now at the ANQQ Picture Library.

138. Bellerive, *op. cit.*, pp. 31–32.

139. ANQQ, 1871 Census, District No. 143, sub-district of Pointe-aux-Trembles, family 245, line 15.

140. At about the same time, on June 18, 1869, *La Minerve* reprinted (p. 2) a glowing article from *Le Courrier du Canada* noting that "age had in no way diminished the talents of the artist," adding this illuminating comment: "Having retired for some time to the country to enjoy greater peace and quiet and, at the same time, to satisfy his love for horticulture, he continued to cultivate his art, on which he spent all his spare time, especially in the winter months."

141. *Le Courrier du Canada*, November 10, 1869, p. 2. These works were among the nine large paintings by Plamondon that were destroyed in the Saint-Jean-Baptiste fire in June 1881. Five other paintings, including four small medallions, were saved from the flames. See *Saint-Jean-Baptiste de Québec. Album publié à l'occasion du 50ᵉ anniversaire de l'érection canonique de la paroisse et du jubilé d'or de Mgr J.-E. Laberge, curé*, Québec City, L'Action catholique, 1936, pp. 136–138.

142. *Le Journal de Québec*, November 18, 1869, p. 2. A concert was also organized in his honour in December. *Le Courrier du Canada*, December 15, 1869, p. 3.

143. *Le Courrier du Canada*, January 3, 1870, p. 2.

144. *Le Courrier du Canada*, July 1, 1870.

145. *Le Journal de l'Instruction publique*, September 1871, p. 120; *Le Courrier du Canada*, September 13, 1871, p. 1; *L'Événement*, September 13, 1871, p. 1. About the portrait of Pius IX, see Mario Béland, "Acquisitions récentes", *Cap-aux-Diamants*, Vol. 3, No. 4 (Winter 1988), p. 72.

146. *Le Courrier du Canada*, September 16, 1874, p. 3. The painting went on display at Québec's provincial exhibition in 1877. *Le Nouvelliste*, September 21 and 27, 1877, p. 2. The painting, which is in very poor condition, is now at the Musée d'art de Joliette. It is based on an engraving that appeared in *L'Opinion publique* on November 6, 1873.

147. *Le Canadien* quoted in *La Minerve*, June 6, 1874, p. 2.

148. *Le Journal de Québec*, November 21, 1874, p. 2.

149. *Le Journal de Québec*, November 26, 1874, p. 2.

150. *Le Journal de Québec*, December 16, 1874, p. 2.

151. *Le Courrier du Canada*, August 9, 1877, p. 2.

152. *Le Courrier du Canada*, March 11, 1880, p. 2.

153. Bellerive, *op. cit.*, p. 35; Robert H. Hubbard, *Deux peintres de Québec / Two Painters of Quebec: Antoine Plamondon/1802–1895, Théophile Hamel/1817–1870* (exhibition catalogue), Ottawa, National Gallery of Canada, 1970, pp. 32, 33, 60, and 87.

154. *Le Journal de Québec*, April 1 (p. 2), and September 18, 1884 (p. 2).

155. Hôtel-Dieu du Sacré-Cœur Archives, Québec City, "Journal 1879–1881," February 8 and May 14, 1881 (letter from the artist); "Journal 1881–1884," July 16 and September 24, 1881 (letter from the artist). In October of the following year, Plamondon donated a painting of the *Virgin and Child* as a token of his gratitude to the nuns for having sent him a work in wax. *Idem*, October 30, 1882 (letter from the artist).

156. *Le Courrier du Canada*, March 17, 1871, p. 3; *Le Journal de Québec*, March 23, 1871, p. 3. On January 16, 1877, Plamondon wrote to Bishop Charles-Félix Cazeau (1807–1881), vicar general of the Diocese of Québec City, about painting his portrait from a photograph. Since the artist's remarks are enlightening in more ways than one, we felt it appropriate to quote from it at length: "I recently had the honour of receiving the photograph of your venerable person, as well as your kind letter dated the 9th of this month. / Please accept my most heartfelt thanks. / The likeness appears to be very good, however I regret the fact that the photographer did not print the photograph in a more well-defined and clear manner. Nevertheless, I believe I can make out the features well enough to paint them accurately. / I had the misfortune to paint the late Bishop Baillargeon [*Charles-François Baillargeon (1798–1870)*] from a poor quality photograph, which resulted in a less-than-accurate depiction, leading the Archbishop's entourage to believe that I was no longer capable of painting to the same standard as my portrait of Pope Gregory XVI. However, if they had seen my paintings of Pius IX and a good number of other works, several of which are still in my studio, they would have realized that they are no less accomplished than that of Pope Gregory XVI. / Your portrait, which I shall commence shortly, shall be an excellent opportunity to prove my point, even more so if it were a full-length portrait hanging in an apartment and surrounded by splendid draperies. Alas, I shall be painting only your bust. I shall make every effort to ensure, despite my 74 years, that it is of no lesser quality than that of the good Pope Gregory XVI, […] I remain the most humble servant of the prelate of His Holiness Pius IX. / Antoine Plamondon, History Painter." Archidiocese of Québec City Archives, 61 CD, Neuville, I:70 (letter from Antoine Plamondon to Bishop C.-F. Cazeau, January 16, 1877).

157. *L'Électeur*, January 12, 1883, p. 2; *Le Journal de Québec*, December 26, 1884, p. 2; *La Presse*, March 11, 1885, p. 4. See also Rémi Morissette, *Antoine Plamondon et ses peintures dans l'église de Neuville*, La Société d'histoire de Neuville, 2004, 31 p.

158. *Le Courrier du Canada*, January 8, 1881, p. 2; *L'Électeur*, March 29, 1881. pp. 1–2.

159. *L'Électeur*, December 12, 1884, p. 3; *Le Journal de Québec*, December 26, 1884, p. 2. This donation was conditional on his being allowed to play a piece of music on the organ at Sunday Mass until the end of his days. ANQQ, IBCQ, Antoine Plamondon file. See *Les Chemins de la mémoire*. Tome III : *Biens mobiliers du Québec, op. cit.*, p. 88 (note by Antoine Bouchard).

160. ANQQ, NR, L.-P. Bernard, Deed of gift, July 5, 1883. Among other instruments, Plamondon owned a piano and a harmonium. Pointe-aux-Trembles PA, "Notice biographique…"

161. *Le Courrier du Canada*, February 18, 1885, p. 3. That same year, the June 22 issue of *Le Courrier du Canada* noted a recent visit by the elderly artist to the newspaper's office.

162. *Le Journal de Québec*, December 2, 1886, p. 2; *Le Courrier du Canada*, December 2, 1886, p. 2.

163. *La Presse*, September 16, 1895, p. 6; *La Minerve*, September 17, 1895, p. 4; *Le Monde illustré*, October 19, 1895, p. 370.

164. As a token of appreciation for his generosity, the parish also covered the cost of his funeral service. Pointe-aux-Trembles PA, "Notice biographique…;" Civil registry, September 7, 1895 (burial in the church crypt).

165. See Pointe-aux-Trembles PA, "Notice biographique…"

166. Pointe-aux-Trembles PA, letter from Siméon Alary, a painter in Chicago, to Charles Darveau on September 11, 1917.

167. *Le Courrier du Canada*, March 17, 1871, p. 3; *Le Journal de Québec*, March 23, 1871, p. 3.

168. See *Le Canadien*, August 7, 1833, p. 1; *Le Journal de Québec*, August 2, 1862, p. 2.

169. See *Le Journal de Québec*, February 23, 1850, pp. 2–3.

170. Porter, "Antoine Plamondon (1804–1895) et le tableau religieux…," *op. cit., passim*.

171. *Idem*, p. 21.

172. *Le Courrier du Canada*, March 17, 1871, p. 3.

Catalogue of Exhibited Works

Mario Béland

Studying in Paris

After Titian

This heavily documented painting with a lively history comes from the descendants of the Burroughs family that at one time owned *Lost in the Wood* (1836), a genre scene by Plamondon (see cat. 9), as well as *Virgin with the Chair* after Raphael (undated), also by the same artist.

Plamondon copied *Young Woman at the Mirror* directly from the Titian hanging in the Musée du Louvre. The dimensions and colours of the copy are similar to those of the original. In examining the canvas, a very old restoration to the painting was discovered, perhaps done by the artist himself after the work was shipped from France to Canada. Shortly after the painter's return, the copy was acquired directly from Plamondon by Louis-Joseph Papineau (see cat. 10), probably around 1834 or 1836. When the great patriot was exiled in 1838, the painting was returned to Plamondon before being bought shortly thereafter by Edward Burroughs (1790-1871), and then by his son John (1824-1904), both from Québec City. In mid-February 1845, the Capital's newspapers published an excerpt from a letter in which an English-speaking woman visiting Paris wrote to her family in Québec City, saying, "We were very much delighted at seeing the original of our painting of *Titian's Mistress* in the Palace of the Louvre, in the Galerie Italienne. Ours is a very exact copy by Plamondon, our Canadian artist." According to John Burroughs, the Québec painter "had great affection" for this painting, which he "considered his masterpiece."

Plamondon's Paris training under Jean-Baptiste-Paulin Guérin (1783-1855), dit Paulin-Guérin, Charles X's portrait painter and, in 1828, dean of drawing and painting at the Maison royale de Saint-Denis, left an indelible mark on the Québec artist (see cat. 2). Obviously, the pieces from this training period are very rare today. They include a *Self Portrait*, signed and dated "Paris, 20 mai 1827" (see fig. 3), and *Study of a Woman* (NGC), as well as a few copies after Paulin-Guérin paintings, namely, *Abbé Philippe-Jean-Louis Desjardins* (MAHDQ, with three other versions by Plamondon), the young artist's protector in Paris, and *The Despair of Cain* (see fig. 4). Among the missing works, the dates of which, however, remain uncertain, are the copies of *The Crowning with Thorns* after Titian, and of *The Burial of Atala* after Girodet, two Louvre paintings, and one of *Virgin* and of *Saint Cecilia* after Raphael (see cat. 42). It bears mentioning that, in 1925, Georges Bellerive's claimed that the Québec painter, after studying in Paris, "went to Rome, Florence and Venice to copy a few works from the Italian school at the museums of these cities. He was enchanted by his stay in these different places." However, there is no documented proof that this occurred. Hence, the significance of *Young Woman at the Mirror*, not only for the light it sheds on Plamondon's training in Paris, but also for what it tells us about artistic taste and the practice of copying at the dawn of the 19th century.

Cat. 1
Young Woman at the Mirror, after Titian
Between 1826 and 1830
Oil on canvas, 101 x 82.7 cm
Signed lower right: A. Plamondon
Musée national des beaux-arts du Québec, purchase (95.07)
Conservation treatment by the Centre de conservation du Québec

Québec City Period
1830-1850

Influence of a Former Master

In this admirable portrait, one of Plamondon's best-known works in Québec, the artist depicts a young student dutifully writing at his work table. The subject is none other than Cyprien Tanguay (1819-1902), 12 years old at the time and halfway through his secondary-level studies at the Séminaire de Québec. He is dressed in the institution's official uniform, a navy blue coat with white piping, adorned, in this case, with a lace jabot and a ruff of irregular design. Two years later, Plamondon would do a portrait of Honoré Tanguay (see fig. 24), Cyprien's brother, also dressed in the mandatory uniform of the seminarians.

The young boy, set against a dark, plain background, his head lifted, gazing intently at the viewer, with his left fist resting on a work by Cicero, has just finished writing the famous Roman orator's name with a goose quill on a large folded sheet of paper. A pewter inkwell and two other books, unidentified, piled one on top of the other, are also on the table's green baize. The right arm on a slant, the striking brightness of the white sheet, and the pile of books, also placed diagonally, interrupt and galvanize the balance and harmony of this triangular and highly classical composition.

Art historian Gérard Morisset penned the following about *Cyprien Tanguay*: "In this portrait, [Plamondon] breaks free from the fetters of his master Guérin." However, this is not the case because the cropping of the painting and the pose of the young student are directly derived from a well-known work by Paulin-Guérin, a portrait of priest and writer Félicité Robert de Lamennais (1782-1854) (fig. 16) done in 1826, the same year the Québec painter took up with his Parisian master. However, in his transposition, Plamondon distances himself somewhat from Guérin by presenting his model face-on rather than turned at a three-quarter angle, by removing the chair, and by adding accessories. Among other notable changes, the rigour and seriousness of the French thinker have given way to the freshness and innocence of the Canadian pupil.

Fig. 16
Jean-Baptiste-Paulin Guérin, dit Paulin-Guérin (1783-1855),
L'Abbé Félicité Robert de Lamennais (artist copy also conserved at the Musée national du Château et des Trianons de Versailles), 1826;
oil on canvas, 81 x 65 cm. Musée des Beaux-Arts de Pau, France (894.16.1).

Above and beyond illustrating how Plamondon both borrowed and drifted away from the conventions of Québec painting of the era, the portrait of Cyprien also portrays a key activity in a student's classical education—instruction in the great Greco-Roman authors of antiquity through the study of Latin. This two-pronged approach in which a portrait also depicts an interrupted activity would not be used very often by Plamondon (see cat. 11 and 28). But, most importantly, this sensitive and spontaneous portrait adumbrates the serious and studious seminarian with a brilliant future as an eminent historian. Ordained a priest in 1843 and appointed rector to various parishes, Cyprien Tanguay would go on to become one of the most learned and renowned archivists and genealogists of his time through works that included his monumental *Dictionnaire généalogique des familles canadiennes-françaises* (1871-1890).

Cat. 2
Cyprien Tanguay
1832
Oil on canvas, 73 x 59.9 cm
Signed and dated lower right: Ant. Plamondon / pinxit 1832
Musée de la civilisation, Séminaire de Québec Collection (1991.74)

Portrait of a Military Man

From the time he returned from France until the time he moved to Neuville, in 1851, Plamondon laid claim to the lion's share of the portrait market in Québec City. In addition to what was called "family subjects" (parents and their children), the painter's clientele hailed from various echelons of Canadian society—politicians, members of the liberal professions, merchants and seigneurs, as well as men of the cloth and military men.

This portrait of a soldier was signed by Plamondon in 1832, two years after he settled in Québec City. From this point on, the artist's reputation as a portraitist would be sealed. As *The Quebec Gazette* reported on December 13, 1833, the Reverend Daniel Wilkie (around 1777-1851), in an address to the Literary and Historical Society of Québec, was especially lavish in praising the virtuosity of Plamondon's portraits of military men:

> Above all, I would recommend to military men a sitting to Mr. P's pencil; for his "soldier likenesses" are really *chef d'œuvres*, displaying as they do so much of the characterizing spiritual touch & splendour of the colouring. Even in the minor essential of such portraits he is astonishingly great—the very epaulettes he paints being absolute pictures in themselves seeming to shine in all the bright and gorgeous splendour of their golden reality.

Until very recently, none of Plamondon's military portraits had been found, the painter's clients having no doubt taken them back with them to England after their years garrisoned in Québec City. So here is the first work of this genre. Since the quality of its composition and manner are exceptional, this painting displays for us the full breadth of the artist's abilities in this field. This portrait, whose history and provenance are unclear, is of Charles Campbell (1792-1872), the son of a Loyalist and a lieutenant-colonel in the famous 99th Regiment of Foot of the Prince of Wales, assigned to North America at the time.

Charles Campbell did border duty near Lake Champlain and in the Niagara Peninsula during the Anglo-American War of 1812-1814. Made lieutenant in 1814, he married Harriet Doxey in 1818, while he was posted in Montréal. With his brothers Archibald (see fig. 19) and John Saxton, he became one of the founding members of the Literary and Historical Society of Québec, created in 1824 under the aegis of Lord Dalhousie. Five years later, he commissioned the construction on Grande Allée of a sprawling two-story Palladian villa flanked by two lateral wings, Battlefield Cottage, directly on the Plains of Abraham (the current site of the Dominican monastery).

This neoclassical portrait, of undeniable artistic merit, is an eloquent witness to the young artist's Paris training under his master Paulin-Guérin, himself known for his many portraits of high-ranking officers of the French army and navy (Château de Versailles and Musée de l'armée de Paris). Very well-off financially and at the peak of his career, Campbell, aged 40, is dressed in his Captain's uniform, with its idiosyncratic thick epaulette fringes and the red suit buttons bearing the number 99 beneath a British crown. The company officer, his right thumb between two uniform buttons, is portrayed from the waist up, standing in front of flowing greenish draperies that counterbalance the vermilion suit with yellow cuffs and collar and the landscape sketched on the right, in keeping with the spirit of English portraiture. The landscape depicted is one of Campbell's favorite views, taken from Battlefield Cottage as he looks out towards the cliffs on the south shore of the St. Lawrence River and, in the distance, the Appalachian Mountains, slightly exaggerated. This is the first and practically the only instance of the artist portraying a clearly identified vista (see cat. 29). But, above all, this finely honed painting could have doubled as a visiting card for the "Student of the French School" in approaching an English-speaking clientele.

Cat. 3
Captain Charles Campbell
1832
Oil on canvas, 91.5 x 76.5 cm
Signed and dated lower left: Ant. Plamondon / 1832
Private collection, Montréal

Merchants and Seigneurs

In the early 1830s, Plamondon attracted a number of clients from the merchant class of the Lower St. Lawrence region, such as Pierre Pelletier (1793-1843), originally from Sainte-Anne-de-la-Pocatière, a trader in Lower Town Québec City, and Amable Dionne (1781-1852), a Kamouraska businessman and major landowner. Plamondon also did the portrait of Dionne's wife, née Catherine Perrault (1787-1875), and that of one of her relatives (MNBAQ, 34.508).

At the time, the artist did bust portraits conceived according to a simple, sober, very direct and almost austere approach to the model. Various conventions contribute both to the intimacy and consistency of these compositions: frontality; tight cropping; very close foreground; neutral, subtly nuanced background; and the lighting focused on the face; elements which intensify the subjects' expressions which are simultaneously intense, calm and natural. In his portraits of men, the permutations of the colour white in the shirt, collar and cuffs contrast with the dark tones of the suit, but in his paintings of women, it is the stylish garb and hairdo consisting of wide curls that give the artist an opportunity to display his talent. The strokes range from finely detailed, as in the model's face, to broad, as in the clothing and accessories. By studying the painting with the naked eye, we are privy to the process of its creation. For the Dionne portraits, we see a drawing beneath the layer of paint, and for that of Mrs. Dionne, pentimenti in the positioning of the collar and the left shoulder. In another vein, Plamondon delivers a discerning analysis of the personality of his models—a headstrong Pelletier, an authoritarian Dionne and a kindly Mrs. Dionne. Newly moneyed merchants and rich seigneurs exude confidence, if not self-sufficiency, the look of self-made men, pleased with their financial, social and professional success.

Cat. 5
Amable Dionne
1834
Oil on canvas, 68.8 x 56.6 cm
Musée national des beaux-arts du Québec,
gift of the Honourable Alexandre Taschereau (34.507)
Conservation treatment by the Centre de conservation du Québec

Cat. 6
Mrs. Amable Dionne, née Catherine Perrault
1834
Oil on canvas, 68.8 x 56 cm
Signed and dated centre right: A. Plamondon / 1834
Musée national des beaux-arts du Québec,
gift of the Honourable Alexandre Taschereau (34.506)
Conservation treatment by the Centre de conservation du Québec

Re-elected the Member of Parliament for Kamouraska in 1834, the year of his portrait and that of his wife, Amable Dionne, seigneur of La Pocatière and of des Aulnaies and major in the militia, endorsed the Ninety-two Resolutions asserting the demands of the House of Assembly and its grievances against the British government. Note that it was Pierre Pelletier who commissioned the masterly portrait of his daughter, Marie-Louise-Émilie, who became Sœur Saint-Alphonse, painted by Plamondon in 1841 (see fig. 9). Through their orders or purchases, Pelletier and Dionne also encouraged other painters, the American James Bowman and Joseph Légaré in the case of the former, and Théophile Hamel and Antoine-Sébastien Falardeau in the case of the latter.

Cat. 4
Pierre Pelletier
Between 1830 and 1835
Oil on canvas, 73 x 60.3 cm
Musée national des beaux-arts du Québec, purchase (54.44)

According to the last owners of this painting published and exhibited for the first time ever, *Saint Francis Xavier Preaching in India* may have come from Plamondon's Neuville studio. We therefore know nothing about the circumstances of its production. However, we do know that the iconography of this composition was based on an anonymous painting imported from France in 1733 by the Parish of Saint-François-Xavier-de-Batiscan (deposited in the collection of the MNBAQ). We propose the early 1830s as the tentative date of this artist copy. This medium-size, finely executed practice copy, probably painted directly from the prestigious Batiscan model, would become in turn an iconographic source for other large church paintings by Plamondon. The artist used this composition several times, for example, in the Parish of Saint-Jean, île d'Orléans, in 1833, of Saint-Augustin-de-Portneuf the following year (now at the NGC), and of Saint-Charles-de-Bellechasse in 1852 (or 1859).

Canonized in 1622, François Xavier (1506-1552), a Spaniard, and co-founder of the Society of Jesus with Ignatius of Loyola, is famous for his missionary work in India and is among the most representative saints of the Counter Reformation. As the second patron saint of Canada, Saint Francis Xavier was particularly venerated, mainly due to the movement known as the Propagation of the Faith, of which he was the figurehead, and to the novena in honour of him. It comes as no surprise, then, that throughout the 19th century, evangelization scenes were extremely popular in Québec. In fact, the composition painted by Plamondon depicts the Jesuit converting the Indians. Dressed in a cassock and an ample surplice, he holds the crucifix received from Saint Ignatius.

From the outset of his career in Québec City, Plamondon earned a reputation as an excellent copyist. As a result, copies of religious paintings would play a central role in his production and contribute to his renown as an artist during this period, much more than his portraits, which today are more highly sought by collectors and museums alike.

Cat. 7
Saint Francis Xavier Preaching in India, after an unknown artist
Between 1830 and 1835
Oil on canvas, 183.5 x 119.5 cm
Signed in lead pencil on the reverse side of the canvas, upper right:
A Plamondon p.
Musée national des beaux-arts du Québec, purchase (68.06)
Conservation treatment by the Centre de conservation du Québec

Portrait of a Clergyman

This portrait of Abbé David-Henri Têtu (1807–1875), from the model's family, may have been commissioned by a close relative of the then 28-year old priest who had been the rector of Saint-Roch de Québec since 1833. The portrait is fully consistent with the physical description of the subject handed down by his vicar, Charles Chiniquy (1809–1899):

> He had a very beautiful appearance: tall and well-proportioned, wide forehead, blue eyes, a remarkably handsome nose, red lips. He had very white skin, even too white for a man, but his short sideburns corrected what could have been too feminine in his face and gave his entire person both a virility and pleasantness.

Plamondon executed many portraits of members of the high and low clergy (see cat. 29), including that of Chiniquy himself in 1842. Simply composed but powerfully evocative, the portrait of this educated city-dwelling priest nonetheless differs in a number of respects from the other portraits of clergymen done during this period. It is one of the rare portraits by Plamondon in which the subject is portrayed upright and cropped mid-thigh (see cat. 16), against a full backdrop of flowing red drapes. The young pastor's left hand is on a pile of books that includes *Imitation de Jésus-Christ* and *Histoire sainte*, near which are sheets of paper, an inkwell, and a quill, the distinguishing accessories of a classically educated member of the secular clergy.

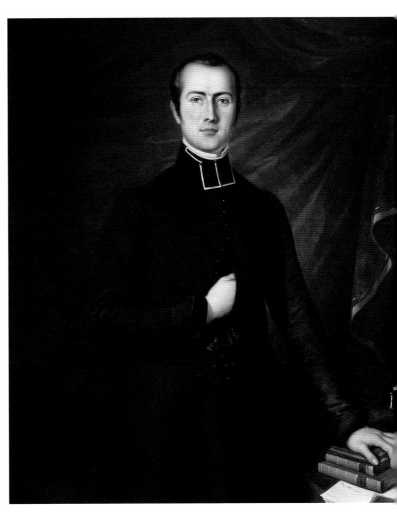

Cat. 8
Abbé David-Henri Têtu
1835
Oil on canvas, 122 x 101.5 cm
Signed and dated lower right (on the parchment):
Ant. Plamondon pinxit / 1835
National Gallery of Canada, Ottawa, purchased in 1966 (14895)

Fantasy Painting

1836 was a pivotal year in Plamondon's career. After six years in Québec City, he set up shop in Montréal from June to October, and offered his services in the June 27 issue of *La Minerve* for "portraits, church works, genre scenes, fantasy pictures, etc." It was probably in Montréal that Plamondon produced *Lost in the Wood*, one of his first genre scenes, that would eventually end up in the hands of the Burroughs family of Québec City (see cat. 1). Unfortunately, little is known about the circumstances surrounding the execution of this singular painting and its acquisition by the Burroughs.

The touching adventure portrayed by Plamondon bespeaks innocence that could not help but satisfy the era's sensibilities. The painter himself was fond of this secular genre, as evinced by his other fantasy pieces in which children are depicted in an outdoor setting (see cat. 33). This kind of anecdotal imagery that is far from devoid of sentimentality is based on folk tales and stories, highly prized by the bourgeoisie and, consequently, widely disseminated in various forms of illustrations. It is therefore entirely plausible that the artist was inspired by such literary or iconographic sources for this composition, as he was for his other genre scenes without exception (see cat. 27 and 33).

Be that as it may, here Plamondon is ingenious in attracting full attention to the children, placed in the middle of a glade suffused with twilight. The artist accentuated the picturesque, if not romantic, nature of the scene through the sharp contrasts between the various planes, which are, by turns, painstakingly detailed or blurrily indistinct, and through the complex interplay of dark and light tones. All these conventions converge to help make the illustration effective and, by the same token, to convey the emotional charge of the event experienced by the two children, lost in the wood.

Cat. 9
Lost in the Wood, likely after an unknown artist
1836
Oil on canvas, 74 x 64 cm
Signed and dated lower left (on a rock):
A. Plamondon / fecit. 1836.
Musée national des beaux-arts du Québec, purchase (82.14)

Emblematic Figures

In Montréal in the summer of 1836, Plamondon enjoyed such success that he could not keep up with demand. His major achievements included the portrait of the popular leader of the *Patriote* party and Speaker at the House of Assembly, Louis-Joseph Papineau (1786-1871), as well as those of his wife, née Julie Bruneau (1795-1862), and of their eldest daughter, Ézilda (1828-1894). Given the prestige of the commission—Papineau was at the pinnacle of his political career at the time—Plamondon pressed all of his know-how into service in order to produce portraits as ambitious as they were innovative, in terms of the carefully weighted cropping, the refinement of the decor, and the richness of the clothing and accessories.

The two paintings, forming a diptych of sorts, go hand in hand. In keeping with the tradition of French portraits of royalty and the aristocracy, the rich bourgeois face each other, seated sideways in an armchair in front of heavy canopied red drapes. In this triple two-part portrait, the man is centred in the composition, whereas the woman, because of the presence of her young daughter to the right, is positioned more towards the left, the two parents counterposed asymmetrically in an altogether particular dynamic.

Louis-Joseph Papineau is wearing his long black Speaker's robe that contrasts with the whiteness of the jabot and the double lawyer's bands. In his left hand, he is holding a book upright against his thigh, and in his right, a sheet of paper with handwriting unrolled on a table. Near the document, richly bound books whose authors are intended as political paradigms (Aristotle, Demosthenes, Montesquieu, Jefferson, etc.) are piled haphazardly beside an ornate inkwell tray. This set of items is positioned against an overflowing bookshelf sketched in the background. Plamondon's dramatization is clearly indicative of the ambitions of the famous orator, eager to project the image of a highly cultivated statesman of eminent stature. When the painter returned to Québec City, the October 10, 1836, issue of *Le Canadien* affirmed without reserve that "Mister Plamondon was the first to give us a good portrait of the great patriot."

It is worthwhile pointing out that the picture of Mrs. Papineau with her daughter, both of whom are bedecked in their best finery, is Plamondon's only portrait that depicts a mother and her child, a type of portrayal in which his student and future competitor, Théophile Hamel, would later excel. This interrupted music lesson shows Julie Bruneau holding a small sheet of music on which is written the name Ézilda, while her eight-year-old daughter turns her head towards the viewer, smiling mischievously. Shadowed in the background are a lyre and a charming bouquet, two symbolic elements that round out the decor.

The two paintings, the elements of their compositions contrasting and complementing each other in an eloquent pictorial dialogue, constitute a decisive moment in the Canadian art of the time. The two distinct spaces and two complementary settings allude to the political, professional and public world on the one hand, and to family, domestic and private life on the other, the comfortable living room contrapuntal to the office; the extravagance of the dresses, to the austerity of the robe; the piano, to the desk; the lyre and the bouquet, to the bookshelf; and, lastly, the sheet music, to the legal tome. The man, in his desire to affirm his worth, seems subordinated to the responsibilities arising from his position and functions, just as the wife reveals herself to be confined to the role of mother and educator, while exhibiting sensitivity to pœtry and the recreative arts. Given the classical and official composition of the portraits and the weightiness of appearances and bourgeois conventions, the two adults take great care to hide their character, thereby coldly distancing themselves from the viewer. Here we are worlds removed from the spontaneity and even, the intimacy, that characterize other portraits in which Plamondon managed to better capture the personality of his models.

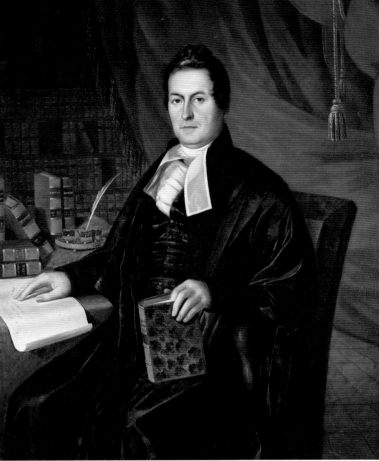

Cat. 11
Mrs. Louis-Joseph Papineau, née Julie Bruneau, and her daughter Ézilda
1836
Oil on canvas, 121.8 x 107 cm
Signed and dated lower left (on the arm of the chair):
A. Plamondon 1836
National Gallery of Canada, Ottawa, purchased in 1974 (17920)

Cat. 10
Louis-Joseph Papineau
1836
Oil on canvas, 122 x 106.8 cm
Signed and dated lower left (on the cloth): A. Plamondon / 1836
National Gallery of Canada, Ottawa, purchased in 1974 (17919)

English-speaking Clientele

During his brief but intense sojourn in Montréal, in 1836, Plamondon took full advantage of the day's demand and the weakness of the competition to produce at least a dozen portraits, among other works. The painter expanded his clientele to the English-speaking business community, as evinced by this remarkable portrait of Mrs. John Redpath. Two years before, Jane Drummond (1815-1907) had married John Redpath (1796-1869), a very well-heeled entrepreneur who made his fortune from his involvement in the construction of the new Notre-Dame church and the Lachine Canal, in Montréal, as well as the Rideau Canal, in Ottawa. Alongside this activity, Redpath was also involved in the city's high finance circles.

It is no surprise, then, to see his second wife in finery of obvious opulence and sophistication: a slate-blue silk dress with generous puffed sleeves, drawn in at the waist by a wide sash, with a sharply pointed cape, accented by various pieces of gold jewelry and, in the curls of her coiffure, a tortoiseshell comb. Sitting slightly to the side, her elbow leaning on the arm of the sofa, Mrs. Redpath holds an octavo in her right hand and, in the other, a crumpled white handkerchief, a bright spot that counterbalances the milky whiteness of her chest.

Here, the pose and gestures are fully consistent with the new approach adopted by the artist in his portraits after 1835. His Montréal portraits mark a transition between the frontal busts of the 1830-1835 period and the family portraits of the 1840s. The models, positioned very high on the canvas, continue to arrest the attention of the viewer, but within a larger frame, with varied poses and expressive gestures. This highly classical construction gives the subjects an air of grandeur while making it possible for the painter to express all his sensitivity in his perception of the characters, as well as his virtuosity in the rendering of fabric and objects.

Cat. 12
Mrs. John Redpath, née Jane Drummond
1836
Oil on canvas, 87 x 73.8 cm
Signed and dated lower left (on the arm of the chair):
A. Plamondon 1836
McCord Museum of Canadian History, Montréal (M994.35.2)

A Prestigious Commission:
The Stations of the Cross *at*
Notre-Dame de Montréal Church

In the summer of 1836, Abbé Joseph-Vincent Quiblier (1796-1852), Superior of the Sulpicians, called on Plamondon to produce the fourteen Stations of the Cross at Notre-Dame de Montréal church. Not only was this the most prestigious commission of the artist's career, but also the most coherent and ambitious series he had ever undertaken. Completed three years later with the help of his apprentices, François Matte and Théophile Hamel, in the fall the monumental work was put on display at the House of Assembly in Québec City, earning its creator lavish praise. But, despite its public and critical success, the Sulpicians were obliged to refuse the fourteen paintings for reasons of religious orthodoxy because some of the Passion scenes did not correspond to the traditional Stations of the Cross. Granted, in Plamondon's defense, it was only in 1820 that devotion to the Stations of the Cross, so popular in Europe, was sanctioned in Lower Canada. The fate of the suite of paintings thereafter was lively, to say the least, until the 1961 acquisition by The Montreal Museum of Fine Arts of six Stations, the rest having disappeared.

The fifth Station, *Jesus Dressed in the Robe of Fools*, signed in 1837, was exposed two years later under the title *Herod Mocked Him, and Arrayed Him in Gorgeous Robe* (see fig. 7). We have found that Université Laval, in Québec City, has a *Histoire de la vie de Jésus-Christ*, a book published in Paris in 1804 that had once belonged to Plamondon's first master, Joseph Légaré, and that includes among its illustrations the same Passion scene with the same title (fig. 17), engraved by Vincent Marie Langlois (1756-after 1796). At the time, the drawing of this etching, like that of many others, was incorrectly attributed to Nicolas Poussin (1594-1665), a French master for whom Plamondon admitted deep admiration. Instead, the representation of the *Robe of Fools* is derived from a composition by the French painter Jacques Stella (1641-1697), taken from a Passion series widely disseminated through engravings. Other compositions reproduced in the same book would be used by Plamondon for his Stations of the Cross, as well as for the famous *Descent from the Cross* after Rubens (see fig. 8).

The fifth Station, as interpreted by Stella, illustrates only the last part of the episode in which Christ is taken to Herod, according to Saint Luke (23, 8-11): "And Herod with his men of war set Him at nought, and mocked Him, and arrayed Him in a gorgeous robe, and sent Him again to Pilate." In his painting, Plamondon changes the various elements of the original representation only slightly, apart from making the

Fig. 17
P. de Ligny, s.j., *Histoire de la vie de Jésus-Christ*, Tome II, À Paris, De L'Imprimerie de Crapelet, 1804, p. 443.
Bibliothèque de l'Université Laval, Québec City, Rare Books (BS-2561-F7-L725-1804).

composition horizontal and reducing it to figures only, at the expense of the interior architecture of the temple, which, in Stella, stretches vertically to occupy most of the space. Clearly, use of an engraved source enabled the painter to showcase his talents as a copyist, but more so as a colourist, as pointed out by an enthusiast in the December 6, 1839, issue of *Le Canadien*: "I would like to pause a moment here to consider not only the expression of the figures, but also and more particularly the use of colour, the beauty of the draperies, their harmony, that of the painting as a whole, on the exactitude and perfection of the drawing."

Cat. 13
Jesus Dressed in the Robe of Fools, after Jacques Stella
1837
Oil on canvas, 152.9 x 240.8 cm
Signed and dated lower right (on the second riser):
A. Plamondon pinxit 1837
The Montreal Museum of Fine Arts,
purchase, Horsley and Annie Townsend bequest (1961.1322)

A tribute to Plamondon's skill and versatility as a copyist, this *Still Life with Grapes* drew compliments from Québec City newspapers. One art connoisseur in the August 24, 1843, issue of *L'Aurore des Canadas* went so far as to say, "Behold how beautiful these grapes are, so juicy that if one were alone and slightly greedy, this small painting would be in grave danger of being munched."

Still life as a genre was a fairly uncommon secular subject in the Canadian painting of the time. Here Plamondon delivers a full and very convincing copy of one of the 70 paintings belonging to Justice Jean-Baptiste-Édouard Bacquet (1794-1853) of Québec City. This canvas, formerly attributed to Campidoglio, has now been established as that of an artist who worked in Rome in the mid-17th century. It is likely that Plamondon studied *Vines and Grapes* for his own pleasure, and not because it was commissioned, relishing the technical challenges it posed in the colouring of the leaves and grapes and the contrast of light and shadow. In fact, we can detect brush strokes under the current surface that may be touch-ups or even pentimenti. Joseph Légaré, Plamondon's first master, produced two copies of this work, one of which was very faithful to the original (between 1843 and 1848, MNBAQ), and the other, horizontal, and with the still life placed in a landscape (before 1826, NGC).

Cat. 15
Unknown artist, Italy, 17th century
Vines and Grapes
Around 1650
Oil on canvas, 88.3 x 73.9 cm
Musée de la civilisation, Séminaire de Québec Collection (1991.206)

Cat. 14
Still Life with Grapes, after an unknown artist
1838
Oil on canvas, 91.7 x 75 cm
Signed and dated lower left: Plamondon / 1838
Musée national des beaux-arts du Québec, purchase (76.175)
Conservation treatment made possible through a contribution by the Amis du Musée national des beaux-arts du Québec

A Portrait Allegorical and Mythical

In April 1838, during an extremely productive period, Plamondon presented a portrait entitled *The Last of the Hurons* for an annual contest on a "national" theme, organized by the Literary and Historical Society of Québec, for which he won the first-class medal "for an original work." Plamondon's resounding success was to be echoed in the Québec City and Montréal press. But, ironically, his greatest triumph would be the purchase of his highly exotic painting by John George Lambton (1792-1840), 1st Earl of Durham, new governor-general of the British North American colonies and author of the eponymous report that contained an unfortunate reference to a French Canadian people without history or literature. Five months after his arrival in Québec City, on May 29, Lord Durham returned to London with the canvas, removing it from the gaze of Canadians for the next 145 years or so.

Plamondon's painting was therefore produced and received in the wake of the tumult of the *Patriote* uprising, in a time of fierce ideological, political and cultural unrest. This lengthy excerpt from the *Canadien* of April 30, 1838, speaks volumes about the climate of uncertainty and anxiety about the future of the French Canadian nation:

> Mr. Plamondon won this token of esteem by reproducing on canvas with all the grace and naturalness of his brilliant palette the features of the last purebred Huron Indian to live in this Province [...] The last of the Hurons! That in itself is an interesting, artistic and truly Canadian subject and Mr. Plamondon took full advantage of it. He has depicted his savage standing in an imposing, warrior-like and meditative manner, his arms crossed on his breast, his forehead raised to the sky; he has placed him in the middle of his woods, to which he seems to be saying a final, solemn farewell, for himself and for his entire race; in a word, he has truly painted the last of the Hurons. When one gazes [...] on his long black flowing hair, curling on his shoulders, his eminently characteristic features, his coppered flesh, his sparkling eyes, the beautiful fabric of his coat, his sash from which his cutlass hangs, one recognizes him for the son of *free men* [...] the last offshoot of a noble and intrepid nation, which has disappeared before our very eyes [...] as perhaps we ourselves will also disappear, giving way to a more powerful nation. The strong hunt the weak [...] It is to be hoped that this gentleman [Plamondon] will not stop there, that our beautiful country will yield up other subjects no less picturesque [...] May all our fellow countrymen work in this way, each in his own field! May we raise some monuments of ourselves before we are engulfed in a wave of immigration! Then we would no longer ask ourselves: when will the day come when Canada emerges from its obscurity, and when will arts and science flourish here as elsewhere? Let us admit it frankly, although our national future is very uncertain, there is much hope for us yet [...]; who knows whether we will one day point as other peoples to our glorious authors, learned people and artists. Courage! And onward young Canadians.

This creed of survival, stirred up by fear of the assimilation of French Canadians in North America, would be repeated just as metaphorically in a long poem by historian François-Xavier Garneau (1809-1866), published in *Le Canadien* of August 12, 1840, and, inspired by the portrait by Plamondon, appropriately entitled «Le Dernier Huron». Since its repatriation from England in 1982, we have been able to measure the impact of the brief presence of this canvas in Québec City in 1838 and its lasting impression.

The portrait of Zacharie Vincent (1815-1886), a young Amerindian unlike any of the artist's usual portrait clients, is unique among Plamondon's prolific repertoire. The subject is placed outdoors, radiant against very dark foliage and, in the distance, rolling hills at sunset, an obvious reference to the relatedness of Native peoples, untamed nature, and the day drawing to a close. Except for the versions of *The Flutist* (see cat. 34, 35 and 37), to our knowledge there is only one other portrait, which, incidentally, dates from the same period, that of Louis de Lagrave painted in 1836 (MMFA), in which the figure, in keeping with the tradition of English portraiture, is depicted in a natural setting without any other devices. The portrait of Vincent is also different because of the cropping and the pose of the model, portrayed standing up and cut off at mid-thigh, a rare choice for Plamondon (see cat. 8). Furthermore, and for the first and only time, the subject crosses his arms and does not look out at the viewer. Clearly, the artist's purpose here is not to paint a simple ethnographic and conventional portrait of an Amerindian, but rather to bequeath to posterity a type as part of a genuine, romantically inspired allegory. For his part, Zacharie Vincent Telari-o-lin (meaning "unmixed" or "bilingual"), who became a very popular symbol as the last survivor of his race, would go on to be immortalized by other famous painters and photographers of his time. The "last of the purebred Hurons," well aware of his status and image, would produce some ten Primitive folkloric self portraits after taking a few painting lessons from none other than Antoine Plamondon.

Cat. 16
The Last of the Hurons [*Zacharie Vincent*]
1838
Oil on canvas, 114.3 x 96.5 cm
Signed and dated on the reverse side of the canvas (before rebacking):
Le Tableau est le Portrait du dernier des Hurons de Lorette, il se nome
Zacarie Vincent, il est agée de 23, Peint par Ant Plamondon à québec 1838.
Private collection, Toronto

Marie-Louise Dallaire, the 20-year-old daughter of Lévis merchant Étienne Dallaire (1796-1866), married Joseph Laurin (1811-1888) on September 3, 1839. The author of five scholarly works, Laurin became a notary on August 20 of the same year, just before his marriage. Indisputably, the portrait of Marie-Louise Dallaire was done on the occasion of her wedding.

Seated on a chair, but, strangely enough, seeming to be standing, Miss Dallaire, smiling faintly, rests her left hand on her midriff. Tightly cropped, the subject dominates the entire surface of the canvas, and, despite her youth, is remarkably forceful. The woman is dressed in her finest attire: a shimmering taffeta dress with leg-of-mutton sleeves and a pleated bodice, a mantilla in chiffon embroidered with vegetal designs, a lace bonnet adorned with ribbons and flowers, and, of course, the attendant jewelry in abundance. Plamondon takes this opportunity to once again give viewers a feast for the eye. His technique in re-creating the tactility of the fabric using broad strokes is consummate, as is his sophisticated sense of colour. There is no question that the portrait of Marie-Louise Dallaire, infused with innocence and freshness, is further proof of Plamondon's remarkable mastery of his art. It also marks the transition from his busts of the 1830s and his seated models leading up to the 1840s. Two years later, when he produced his portrait of Joseph Laurin (MNBAQ), the painter opted this time for a broader frame within which the subject, cropped at the waist, is depicted standing in front of wide draperies.

Cat. 17
Mrs. Joseph Laurin, née Marie-Louise Dallaire
1839
Oil on canvas, 84.6 x 71.3 cm
Musée national des beaux-arts du Québec, purchase (64.51)

At the Peak of his Art

In the early 1840s, Plamondon and some art enthusiasts constructed a new aesthetic discourse around portraiture, based not so much on its likeness-to-life as on the artistic qualities of the work per se. The painter and commentators therefore emphasized the technical ability to conjure up both the living essence of the model and the presence of matter in the rendering of clothing and objects.

In 1841, during his stint as a drawing instructor at the Hôpital Général de Québec, Plamondon produced, along with his portrait of Sœur Saint-Alphonse (see fig. 9), two admirable portraits of nuns from this congregation, Sœur Saint-Joseph (fig. 18) and Sœur Sainte-Anne, commissioned by their parents. The daughters of Joseph Guillet dit Tourangeau (see cat. 19) and of Judith Kimner dit Laflamme (see cat. 20), the girls were christened Flore and Marie-Mathilde. Sœur Saint-Joseph, who died prematurely at age 30, had a short career, but Sœur Sainte-Anne set a record for longevity in the Augustine community. As indicated on the label on the reverse side of the canvas, she entered the postulate on May 28, 1840, took the veil on October 17, and her final vows on October 21 of the following year. She remained in the community until her death at the venerable age of 85. Like her sister, she taught drawing and performed other duties in the residence of the institution.

Painted by Plamondon with sensitivity and consummate skill, these portraits of nuns are all composed according to the artistic principles and formal conventions of neoclassicism. Positioned in front of a shimmering background, the cloistered nuns, seated at an angle in an armchair, looking away from the painter, seem enveloped in a diffuse, ethereal, almost supernatural light. Thanks to the artist's adept handling of light, the portraits spring to life, imbued with a strong physical presence and intense spirituality.

At least, this is how "a friend of painting," Joseph-Édouard Cauchon (see fig. 13), the editor of *Le Canadien* and Plamondon's mentor, interpreted the portraits of nuns by Plamondon, in a long dithyrambic article published on August 20, 1841:

Fig. 18
Sœur Saint-Joseph, 1841; oil on canvas, 91.8 x 74.5 cm; signed and dated lower right (on the arm of the chair): A. Plamondon 1841. Musée des Augustines de l'Hôpital Général de Québec (2002-950).

The portraits he has just completed are of a type quite different from ordinary portraits and [...] the artist has had to achieve his effects by other means [...] The painter had to overcome great difficulties, especially in regard to the face, which is almost entirely covered by a wide, tight band, which pulls together and constricts the forehead and cheeks, depriving them of that graceful openness and the freedom which the painter so delights to depict and the viewer to admire. [...] The problems to be surmounted were immense, since the face necessarily occupies a position of prime importance in a portrait, and the remainder is but an accessory. Endeavouring always to bring out the relief [...], he never portrays his subjects full face, [...] but rather at a two-third or three-quarter turn. [...] Without the oblique lighting entailed in painting the face at an angle there would be no contours or relief, and hence no mystery [...] In these portraits you will see magnificent contrasts of light and shade; however [...], you will be unable to determine precisely where the two divide because the painter has moulded his contours, modifying his colours by imperceptible extremes of light and shade [...] What beauty there is in this costume! How naturally and impulsively he has clothed his subjects! What freedom there is in the folds of the mantle! What grace and what finesse of outline! What suppleness! What flowing sleeves! And how soft and marvelous the diaphanous veil; the illusion is perfect, you want to reach out and touch the garments. Although the artist had to reproduce the same costume in the three portraits, he has achieved a variation in his treatment by a differentiation in the folds, and in the effects of light and shade. One difficulty which the painter had to deal with [...] is the monotony of the poses [...] they are dignified, and [...] the subjects are sitting so naturally, and with such ease, that they seem to be unaware that they were posing for their portraits [...] Now that you have considered the portraits as a whole, come closer and examine the details. Note the care used in the execution; see if you can find the traces of a brushstroke [...] see how the painter has caught the moistness of the eye, the tear just emerging from the tear duct, the crystalline transparency of the cornea, without which the painting would be nothing—for the artist would have failed to create [...] life-like realism [...] Mr Plamondon's use of colour—which is the most impressive aspect of his talent—is the best on this side of the ocean.

Mentioned in the Cauchon article of August 20, but signed only next September 10, the portrait of Sœur Sainte-Anne reveals features similar to those of her father, but also bespeaks strong will, attentiveness and intelligence. The young 18-year-old nun wears the white veil of the novice, which, needless to say, illuminates the entire canvas. In addition, this wide veil gives the composition its pyramidal and balanced structure, along with its density and monumentality. All the white parts of the habit—the veil, headband, rochet and robe—are foils for the black solidity of the cope, thus allowing the portraitist to display his virtuosity in his treatment of the fabric. The nuances and harmony of the palette, with its subtle shades ranging from pristine white to a spectrum of beiges to ebony, contribute wholly to the powerful illusion of the fullness of the habit, with its folds that are flowing and heavy by turns, in keeping with the nature of the material. Add to this the softness of the contours, the delicate skin tones, and the fine variations in the artist's rendering of the nun's right hand holding the red book of the *Constitutions* of her order, and it cannot be denied that Plamondon had produced a painting of exceptional quality for that era in Canada.

Cat. 18
Sœur Sainte-Anne
September 10, 1841
Oil on canvas, 88.9 x 71.1 cm
Signed and dated lower right (on the arm of the chair, barely visible):
1841 / A. Plamondon
Musée des Augustines de l'Hôpital Général de Québec (2002-1520)

Members of the Guillet dit Tourangeau and Paradis Families

The dates in bold refer to the dates the paintings were produced.

Parents

Joseph Guillet dit Tourangeau (1794–1855),
January 8, 1842
(MNBAQ, cat. 19),
married at Notre-Dame-de-Québec,
on June 17, 1817,
to

Judith Kimner dit Laflamme (?–?),
1842
(MNBAQ, cat. 20)

François-Xavier Paradis (1798–1862 or 1863),
April 1842
(MNBAQ, cat. 23),
married at Notre-Dame-de-Québec,
on July 9, 1822,
to

Marie-Archange Lacroix (?–?),
1841
(MACM, cat. 24)

Children

Joseph Guillet dit Tourangeau (1818-1893),
March 5, 1842
(MNBAQ, cat. 21),
married at Saint-Charles-Borromée de Charlesbourg,
on September 28, 1841,
to

Caroline Paradis (1823-1908),
daughter of François-Xavier,
June 1842
(MNBAQ, cat. 22)

Flore Guillet dit Tourangeau (1821-1850),
Sœur Saint-Joseph,
1841
(MAHGQ, see fig. 18)

Marie-Mathilde Guillet dit Tourangeau
(1824-1908), Sœur Sainte-Anne,
September 10, 1841
(MAHGQ, cat. 18)

Joséphine Guillet dit Tourangeau (1833-1866),
future Sœur Sainte-Marguerite,
January 1854
(MNBAQ, see cat. 31)

Émilie Guillet dit Tourangeau (1830-1861),
1854
(MNBAQ, see fig. 20),
married at Saint-Roch de Québec,
on November 12, 1851,
to

François-Narcisse Gingras (1825-1877),
1854
(MNBAQ, see cat. 32)

The Guillet and Paradis Families

In October 1842, while visiting Plamondon's studio, Maximilien Bibaud (1823-1887), the editor of *Encyclopédie canadienne*, was struck by the quality of a group of paintings: "Among his bust portraits, my attention was drawn in particular to those of an entire Québec City family, the father, mother, son, daughter, &c. Whether from close up or farther away, it is not only the people themselves that you believe you see, but genuine fabrics, fine drapes, velvet, silk, batiste, lace, ribbons, jewelry, &c."

It is very likely that Bibaud was referring to the portraits of the Guillet dit Tourangeau and Paradis families, painted in 1841 and 1842 by Plamondon, Québec City's most reputable portrait artist of the time. Late in the summer of 1841, the parents of the Guillet and Paradis families commissioned a series of portraits of members of their family to mark certain important events, that is, the marriage of a Guillet son to a Paradis daughter, and two of the Guillet daughters entering religious life. In fewer than two years, a succession of family members appeared before the artist's easel: 48-year-old Joseph Guillet dit Tourangeau Sr., a prosperous baker in Saint-Roch de Québec and a respected citizen, and his wife, née Judith Kimner; his 23-year-old son, also named Joseph, and his 18-year-old wife, née Marie-Adélaïde-Caroline Paradis, married on September 28, 1841; the parents of the latter, 44-year-old François-Xavier Paradis, a highly visible Saint-Roch businessman, and his wife, née Marie-Archange Lacroix. In addition to these three couples, there were two other Tourangeau daughters, Flore and Marie-Mathilde, who, upon entering the Augustine Sisters of Hôpital Général de Québec, took the names Sœur Sainte-Anne (see cat. 18) and Sœur Saint-Joseph (see fig. 18). Twelve years later, in 1854, Plamondon would sign portraits of two other Tourangeau children, namely, Joséphine (see cat. 31) and Émilie (see fig. 20), as well as that of the latter's husband (see cat. 32). In all, the commission from the two families totaled over ten paintings. Worthwhile indeed!

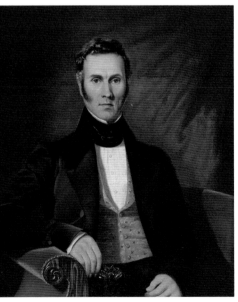

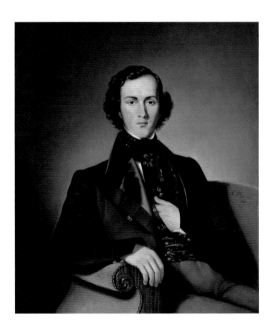

Cat. 19
Joseph Guillet dit Tourangeau, Senior
January 8, 1842
Oil on canvas, 91.5 x 77 cm
Signed and dated lower right
(on the armchair back):
A. Plamondon / 1842
Musée national des beaux-arts du Québec, purchase (53.77)
Conservation treatment by the
Centre de conservation du Québec

Cat. 20
Mrs. Joseph Guillet dit Tourangeau, née Judith Kimner
1842
Oil on canvas, 92 x 76.6 cm
Signed and dated lower right:
A. Plamondon / 1842
Musée national des beaux-arts du Québec, purchase (77.04)

Cat. 21
Joseph Guillet dit Tourangeau, Junior
March 5, 1842
Oil on canvas, 91 x 76.2 cm
Signed and dated centre right
(on the armchair back):
A. Plamondon / 1842
Musée national des beaux-arts du Québec, purchase (56.467)
Conservation treatment by the
Centre de conservation du Québec

Leaving behind his manner of portraiture of the 1830s (see cat. 4 to 6), with this series of canvases Plamondon adopts a new way of cropping his subjects, seated at a three-quarter angle, the men on a sofa, and the women in an armchair, against a plain backdrop, except in the case of the two fathers, where red draperies are used. Apart from the refined costumes and stylish jewelry, there is nothing that points to any profession or function in particular for the subjects, and therefore, nothing to distract the viewer. By giving the subjects "more elbow room" and by using background lighting as a foil, while distancing them from the viewer, the artist had greater leeway to concentrate on the elegance of the figures, the naturalness of the pose, the expression of gestures, the arrangement of the arms and hands, the effect of depth, the richness of textures, the subtle lighting, the finesse of the details and the harmony of the colours. In this way, not only did the artist highlight his subjects by focusing our attention on their physiognomy and facial expressions, but he also made the paintings decorative, giving free rein to his full range of ability. The artistic qualities that combine in these portraits confirm all the confidence gained by Plamondon, who was now in full possession of his means, as well as the social status of these very comfortable bourgeois who are proud of their success, prestige and good taste. The outcome of an entire decade of research, Plamondon's academic and classical approach would also be used by his former pupil, Théophile Hamel, during the same period.

Plamondon would often enjoy the patronage of the members of Québec City's French-speaking middle class, many of whom were close relatives. As 1842 drew to a close, the December 24 issue of *L'Aurore des Canadas* reported: "We have learned […] that several families of distinction had the intention of putting Mr. Plamondon to work, envious as they were of being indebted to the hand of such an expert Canadian artist for the pleasure of seeing their loved ones recreated on canvas for their delight." Five years later, Plamondon would, to paraphrase Napoléon Aubin in *Le Canadien* of October 15, 1847, still be enshrined as the painter *par excellence* of "family subjects."

Cat. 22
Mrs. Joseph Guillet dit Tourangeau,
née Caroline Paradis
June 1842
Oil on canvas, 91.3 x 76.6 cm
Signed and dated lower left:
A. Plamondon / 1842
Musée national des beaux-arts du Québec,
purchase (56.468)
Conservation treatment by the
Centre de conservation du Québec

Cat. 23
François-Xavier Paradis
April 1842
Oil on canvas, 92 x 77 cm
Signed and dated lower right
(on the armchair back):
A. Plamondon / 1842
Musée national des beaux-arts du Québec,
purchase (54.251)
Conservation treatment by the
Centre de conservation du Québec

Cat. 24
Mrs. François-Xavier Paradis,
née Marie-Archange Lacroix
1841
Oil on canvas, 91.5 x 76.8 cm
Signed and dated lower right:
A Plamondon / 1841
Musée d'art contemporain de Montréal,
Lavalin Collection, purchase (A 92 275 P1)

Portraits d'apparat

The years 1841 and 1842, which yielded the portraits of three Hôpital Général nuns, of six members of the Guillet and Paradis families (see cat. 18 to 24), of Joseph Laurin, and of Father Chiniquy and Father Bédard, were undoubtedly the high point of Plamondon's career as a portraitist, in terms of the quantity of commissions and the quality of the paintings. With the Bédard couple, who posed for him during these productive years, the artist reached other heights.

Admitted to the Bar in 1824, Elzéar Bédard (1799-1849) married Julie-Henriette Marett three years later in Québec City. Very early in his career, Bédard become interested in provincial politics. Elected the representative for Montmorency in 1832 and 1834, he joined Papineau's *Patriote* party and presented the famous Ninety-two Resolutions in the House of Assembly. In the meantime, in 1833, he was named the first mayor of the new City of Québec, a position he held for one year. Between 1836 and 1848, Bédard also sat as a judge in Québec City, before dying prematurely in Montréal, in 1849, from the aftereffects of cholera.

With the Bédards, Plamondon primarily repeated, with a few improvements, the artistic devices already proven effective in his portraits of the Papineau couple, painted six years earlier (see cat. 10 and 11). However, this time he relies more heavily on certain effects specific to the *portrait d'apparat*, effects he was, in fact, in the process of exploring in his breathtaking copy of *Pope Gregory XVI* (see fig. 11) by Pietro Gagliardi (1809-1890), a painter from Rome, done at the bishop's palace in Montréal (today's Grand Séminaire).

As with several other portraits of Montréal couples painted in 1836, the two Bédard paintings were not designed only as an absolutely symmetrical pair that could not be separated. In fact, they benefit from being viewed independently. Elzéar Bédard is highlighted using the symbols of his social position and functions. Positioned against wide draperies that partly hide a well-stocked bookshelf, the judge, dressed in his ermine robe over which is a double rabat, is seated, a document in one hand and the other hand elevated, leaning on a book, on his work table, right beside a goose quill dipped in his inkwell. Note that Plamondon would re-use some of the artistic conventions of this painting, namely, the pose, accessories and curtain, in his last large official portrait, that of Senator Joseph-Édouard Cauchon (1816-1885), produced in 1868 (see fig. 13). For her part, Julie-Henriette Marett, with her responsibilities as hostess and mistress of the house, is confined to a role of appearances proper to the wives of the refined and elegant notables from the upper echelons of the society of that era. The young woman, dressed in a ball gown and evening gloves, is seated in a wide armchair. She too is placed in front of draperies, this time, double-tasseled, opening but slightly on a sketchy landscape on the right. It must be granted that, here, the decor and costumes make up for and divert attention from the face, which is not given very much prominence.

The two paintings, harmonious and splendid, are therefore not without the features typical of *portraits d'apparat*, in a professional context in the case of the husband, and, in the case of the wife, a worldly one. This kind of portrait could serve for official and public viewing, as well as for domestic and private enjoyment, such as in an office.

Cat. 26
Mrs. Elzéar Bédard, née Julie-Henriette Marett
1842
Oil on canvas mounted on fibreboard, 123.5 x 98 cm
Signed and dated lower left: A. Plamondon / 1842
Art Gallery of Hamilton,
gift of the Volunteer Committee, 1973 (1969.88.Q)

Cat. 25
Elzéar Bédard
1842
Oil on canvas mounted on fibreboard, 123.5 x 98 cm
Signed and dated lower left: A. Plamondon / 1842
Art Gallery of Hamilton,
gift of the Volunteer Committee, 1973 (1969.88.R)

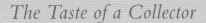

This genre scene grabbed the attention of the editor of *L'Aurore des Canadas* who, after visiting Plamondon's studio, described it in luscious detail in the August 24, 1843, issue of the newspaper:

> *The Little Savoyards*, a pretty work which has just been completed, and which would be enough to make the artist's reputation if he had not already accomplished that long ago […] As always, Mr. Plamondon has imbued the painting with charm and colour, a pœtry of imagination in the painting's background, a beauty and naturalness of character, truthfulness and a happy facial expression…

In *Le Journal de Québec* of next October 3, another admirer of *The Little Savoyards* penned his own lengthy commentary, going so far as to call it "this pleasant piece of a little masterpiece." Dated the following year for some unknown reason, Plamondon's painting was once again the subject of an article, this time in *Le Canadien* of November 19, 1847, which, in this case, provides two critical pieces of information. First, the name of the original owner of the canvas, Denis-Benjamin Viger (1774-1861), a lawyer, journalist, politician and leading Montréal landowner, is mentioned. Viger, you will recall, at the time owned one of the finest collections of paintings in Canada (see cat. 33 and fig. 21). *Le Canadien* also tells us that Plamondon's genre scene was a "delightful copy […] after an engraving of the charming painting by M. Hornung of Geneva, entitled *Happy as a King*, which is known today as *The Little Savoyards*." Unfortunately, we have not been able to find *Happy as a King*—a title taken from a popular expression often associated with drinking songs—by Genevan history and genre painter Joseph Hornung (1792-1870). The Hôpital Général de Québec has an anonymous engraving of *The Little Savoyards* on which Plamondon is likely to have based his copy. The scene depicts orphaned chimneysweeps celebrating after a hard day's work. While clearly inspired by a European work, the subject was meaningful in the colony as well, where, as in Europe, young chimneysweeps often worked in pairs. Plamondon would certainly have included this work in the category he called "genre scenes and fantasy pictures."

Cat. 27
The Little Savoyards, after Joseph Hornung
1844
Oil on canvas, 91.4 x 76.2 cm
Signed and dated lower left: A. Plamondon / 1844
The Montreal Museum of Fine Arts,
gift of Mrs. Alfred Thibaudeau (1963.1393)

Love of Music

Born in La Malbaie, Marie-Adèle Cimon (1831-1886) was the daughter of Hubert Cimon (1789-1854) and Angélique (or Angèle) Simard (1799-1866), a couple whose portrait Plamondon had painted in 1838. It was Hubert Cimon, a very prosperous merchant, lieutenant-colonel in the militia, and justice of the peace, who commissioned the Québec City artist to paint this portrait of Marie-Adèle. The young girl was a boarder at the Ursuline Sisters of Québec City from December 1843 to March 1848. Her uniform makes it possible for us to date production of the portrait to 1848, when she was approximately 17 years old, just before she entered the convent, on March 28, and began wearing the habit of the Ursuline Sisters, next June 20. Marie-Adèle made her perpetual vows on July 18, 1850, taking the name Sainte-Marie, and, in 1863, published a history of the Ursuline Sisters of Québec City, before being appointed superior of her religious community (1872 to 1875).

Plamondon shows us Miss Cimon seated in an armchair, dressed in her plaid frock with a lace collar, the mandatory uniform for Ursuline boarders. At the time, the convent schoolgirl was a musician and even a composer of melodies. She holds pen and paper, beside a table piled with books and sheet music. Plamondon, himself an accomplished musician and, at this point in time, the director of a sacred music ensemble in Québec City, must have been delighted to have this model sit for him. Even though unsigned, this painting is typical Plamondon.

Cat. 28
Marie-Adèle Cimon
1848
Oil on canvas, 97.7 x 81.5 cm
Musée national des beaux-arts du Québec, purchase (81.12)
Conservation treatment by the Centre de conservation du Québec

This unsigned portrait from Saint-Nicolas church depicts Bishop Modeste Demers (1809–1871), born in this parish on the south shore of Québec City. After serving as a missionary priest for the Pacific Coast Amerindians, Abbé Demers was consecrated first bishop of Vancouver Island on November 30, 1847. One year later, on November 10, 1848, *L'Ami de la Religion et de la Patrie* wrote:

> Mr. Plamondon […] has just painted the Bishop of Vancouver. He wishes to preserve this memory of a person with whom he previously had strong ties. We invite painting enthusiasts to come to Mr. Plamondon's studio to view this portrait of which connoisseurs speak so highly, both for its near-perfect likeness and the brilliant colouring for which this gentleman is known.

Plamondon, who had long dominated the portrait market, had been seeking this kind of publicity since Théophile Hamel's return from Europe in 1846. In response to the professional challenge posed by his former pupil, the portrait painter adopted the new approach to the model that Hamel had brought back from Italy and been using since 1847 (fig. 19). Five years earlier, Plamondon had had the opportunity to learn about this new manner of portrait painting when he produced his famous copy of *Pope Gregory XVI* (see fig. 11), a Gagliardi *portrait d'apparat* (now at the Séminaire de Québec).

Against a backdrop of wide green draperies, the subject—clothed in loose-fitting and sumptuous episcopal vestments—is seated in three-quarter profile, with a partly open red missal in his right hand. As with *Pope Gregory XVI*, the generous use of impasto on the sashes, tassels, and golden embroidered ornamentation on the stole catch the light and accentuate the richness of the clothing. When compared to Plamondon's earlier portraits of bishops (Monseigneurs Plessis, Signay, and Turgeon), the composition of the Demers portrait is airier, in part due to the open view of a seascape on the right. The large window shows a small point of land—no doubt an allusion to Vancouver Island—under a dramatic twilight sky. This motif of a glimpse of nature in the Italian manner paired with draperies is rather rare in Plamondon's work, although he had used this

Fig. 19
Théophile Hamel (Sainte-Foy, 1817–Québec City, 1870), *Archibald Campbell*, 1847; oil on canvas, 99.8 x 81.6 cm; signed and dated lower left (on the arm of the chair): T.H. 1847. Musée national des beaux-arts du Québec, purchase (69.358).

formula at the beginning of his career (see cat. 3). While the classical conventions accentuate Bishop Demers' bearing, the expertly rendered portrait, particularly the plump face that exudes both determination and kindness, elicits an appreciation for the keen psychological understanding of the individual—a brilliant and energetic man in the prime of life endowed with a hearty constitution, and a seasoned, multilingual traveler.

Cat. 29
Monseigneur Modeste Demers
1848
Oil on canvas, 114.3 x 94 cm
Musée national des beaux-arts du Québec, purchase (73.35)

The Neuville Period
1851-1885

An Icon of Canadian Painting

In early October 1850 at the first Québec agricultural and industrial exhibition, Plamondon presented a large unfinished painting depicting a pigeon hunt. On October 12, *Le Journal de Québec* gave a description as detailed as it was vivid:

> The painting that attracted the most attention on the part of the many visitors was one of a pigeon hunt, a composition by M. Antoine Plamondon; by the time the judges awarded him first prize, the public had long since awarded him this prize unanimously. The three young hunters are seated on a knoll at the foot of a tree; however, the one behind is standing, pointing out pigeons carelessly perched on the bare branches of a tree to the one holding the weapon. In the latter's hands and all around him are several pigeons already felled by the deadly lead. The subjects are well grouped, and the figures, which are very natural, are extremely mobile. In the painting, there is much perspective, depth, and, most of all, space. The pigeons which we can see in the foreground are painted with such a trueness to life which, in our opinion, is difficult to attain and even more difficult to surpass. Just look at the tiniest details; that horn, for example, and its transparency and the powder that can be seen across it, impress and surprise the onlooker. The colouring of this canvas is like everything that comes from the hands of our artist, rich and true. The trees do not have the polish of the rest, but M. Plamondon, taken by surprise like everyone else, will be able to give his painting the final touches, and especially the varnish, without which the most beautiful work cannot fully satisfy the eye.

The City of Québec hurriedly organized this event with the goal of awarding prizes to samples that would represent the city a few days later at the industrial exhibition in Montréal. Plamondon did not sign his genre painting until three years later, apparently in preparation for another provincial exhibition, again in Montréal, where the work was once again awarded first prize.

In 1865, as reported in the September 1 issue of the newspaper *Le Canadien*, the "magnificent painting" was on display in the window "of the establishment of M.M. Larue and Co." on rue Saint-Jean in Québec City, with a price tag of $500, a tidy sum at the time. The success achieved by the painting, as well as the very high price asked by the merchants, was hardly surprising, given the familiar subject matter and its local flavour, which had all the ingredients for pleasing the Canadian public at the time. Hunting for passenger pigeons—a type of large wood pigeon

(see cat. 37)—was a very popular activity in the St. Lawrence Valley. Too popular, in fact, as it led to the extinction of the species in 1914.

Although the landscape in this studio painting can rightly be connected with Neuville's low-lying plains and the cliffs on the south shore of the St. Lawrence—in addition to being one of the very rare natural settings painted by Plamondon (see cat. 35)—it would be a stretch to claim that the three young hunters were the day labourers hired by the painter around 1851. In fact, it is unlikely, considering that for most of his works of fantasy, Plamondon was systematically inspired by engravings (see cat. 27 and 33). Otherwise, how can we explain the unlikely existence of a composition in his body of work that is so original, structured, dynamic, daring, and demanding in terms of size as well as in terms of the technical challenges posed by the positioning of the figures, the source and direction of the lighting, and the relationship between the foreground and the background and between the figures themselves? In this regard, the contrast between the bleak landscape and the liveliness of the central group, the clothing, the game, and the accessories, is apparent.

Despite the use of an engraving as the source and certain weaknesses in the composition, *The Pigeon Hunt* constitutes not only a landmark painting in the artist's career and production, but also a significant contribution to the creation of a uniquely Canadian iconography. On this point, among Plamondon's most famous works, *Sœur Saint-Alphonse* of the National Gallery of Canada (see fig. 9) has become an icon in the field of portraiture, just as *The Pigeon Hunt* of the Art Gallery of Ontario has become widely known in the field of genre paintings, particularly in English Canada.

Cat. 30
The Pigeon Hunt
1850–1853
Oil on canvas, 184.2 x 182.9 cm
Signed and dated lower left: A. Plamondon / 1853.
Art Gallery of Ontario, Toronto,
gift of the Albert H. Robson Memorial Subscription Fund, in 1943 (2601)

Last Great Portraits

After having painted Guillet dit Tourangeau "father, mother, son, and daughter" (see cat. 19 to 24) in 1841 and 1842, Plamondon received another commission twelve years later from the same family for portraits of their children born later—sisters Joséphine (1833–1866) and Émilie (1830–1861) (fig. 20), as well as for that of Émilie's husband, Francois-Narcisse Gingras (1825–1877), a hardware dealer in Québec City's Lower Town. Following in the footsteps of her sisters Flore and Marie-Mathilde, who became nuns at Hôpital Général de Québec (see cat. 18 and fig. 18), Joséphine decided to join the Ursuline Sisters of Québec City under the name of Mother Sainte-Marguerite on February 2, 1854. This means that her portrait was painted early that year. Encouraged by their father (see cat. 19), who was known for his interest in the arts and notably, as a patron of Joseph Légaré's gallery, both Joséphine and Émilie devoted themselves to the arts—Joséphine to oil painting and Émilie to drawing.

Joséphine, as well as Émilie and her husband, all posed seated in three-quarter profile in the same swan-neck armchair. Joséphine is sitting near a table displaying a beautiful vase of mixed flowers, a rare motif in Plamondon's portraits (see cat. 11) that prefigures his still lifes of the 1870s (see cat. 38 to 40). The three paintings brilliantly reflect the aesthetic of the 1840s in the cropping of the models as well as in the sumptuous treatment of the moiré dresses with their various plays of transparency and colour nuances. This was one of Plamondon's last great moments in portrait painting. With a few rare exceptions—for example, the official portrait of his friend Joseph-Édouard Cauchon (1816–1885) commissioned by the Senate in 1868 (see fig. 13)—the painter from then on limited himself to portraits heavily inspired by photography (see cat. 43), which, while still painted with care, were often dry and stiff.

Cat. 31
Miss Joséphine Guillet dit Tourangeau
1854
Oil on canvas, 91.3 x 76 cm
Signed and dated lower left, vertically: A. Plamondon / 1854
Musée national des beaux-arts du Québec,
gift of Mr. Alexandre Gingras (51.109)

Fig. 20
Mrs. Francois-Narcisse Gingras, née Émilie Guillet dit Tourangeau,
1854; oil on canvas, 92 x 76.5 cm; signed and dated lower left
(on the arm of the chair): A. Plamondon 1854.
Musée national des beaux-arts du Québec, purchase (77.07).

Cat. 32
Francois-Narcisse Gingras
1854
Oil on canvas, 91.3 x 76 cm
Signed and dated lower right, vertically: 1854 A. Plamondon
Musée national des beaux-arts du Québec,
gift of Mr. Alexandre Gingras (51.109)

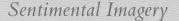

We have no idea whether Plamondon was commissioned to make this painting or whether he painted it simply for his own pleasure. In 1857, the same year this genre painting was signed, *La Minerve* of August 25 reported that, at an exhibition at Bonaventure Hall in Montréal, "We noticed two canvases by Plamondon, including one of truly remarkable taste. It is said to be from the collection of the Hon. D.-B. Viger, who owns another magnificent canvas by the same brush." We have no way of knowing whether *The Little Gardeners* was part of this event. However, it should be noted that, more than ten years earlier, Viger had purchased Plamondon's whimsical piece *The Little Savoyards* (see cat. 27).

For this somewhat unusual painting, Plamondon was inspired by a popular illustration of the time, an engraving entitled *The Little Gardeners* published by G. Baxter Printers of London after a painting by Berliner Eduard Magnus (1799–1872) and published in 1847 in *Marshall's Cabinet of Fashion* and Suttaby's *Le Souvenir*. Plamondon no doubt classified his exact copy of Magnus's work under what he called "genre scenes and fantasy pictures." Although the meaning of this charming scene remains unclear, it exudes a sense of freshness and purity that could not help but appeal to the eclectic tastes of the era. This type of sentimental imagery—rather insipid, it must be said—is the product of the romantically inspired art embraced by Victorian society. Here, Plamondon reflects this nostalgic trend through the innocent, carefree existence of childhood as he did in *Lost in the Wood* (see cat. 9). It should be noted, however, that there is a clear difference, and a shift in direction, in the treatment of the landscape 20 years later. The romanticism of *The Little Gardeners* is portrayed with less dramatic and more diffused lighting using a brighter palette and bolder brush strokes for the foliage.

Cat. 33
The Little Gardeners, after Eduard Magnus
1857
Oil on canvas, 92.7 x 77 cm
Signed and dated lower left: Plamondon / 1857
Musée national des beaux-arts du Québec, purchase (90.68)

Variations on a Theme

As a copyist of religious paintings, Plamondon often experimented with variations on a theme, as in his different versions of the *Miracles of Saint Anne* (see fig. 1). Between 1866 and 1868, the artist did much the same with the secular genre. An avid music lover, Plamondon painted an original composition on the subject of the flutist in at least five fairly different versions. Four of them have been brought together here for the first time. The painter first produced a small vertical composition dated 1866—the Musée national des beaux-arts du Québec version—featuring an adolescent male from mid-thigh up playing a traverse flute against the simple backdrop of a sailing vessel and partially hidden sun on the horizon. Plamondon probably used a studio photograph of a boy, which explains the odd positioning and visual cropping at the legs. An examination of this work for the purpose of conservation treatment revealed a pentimento in the colour (yellow) and placement of the sun (directly on the horizon), as well as modifications in the position of the thighs, right shoulder, and tip of the flute. These changes confirm that this is indeed the first of five versions of *The Flutist*. Our version is followed by the Power Corporation of Canada's horizontal canvas of the same character in the same pose, but now with clearly disproportionate legs. Backlit by a blazing sky, the young man now stands on a large, lone rock set on a whimsical beach; on the water, no fewer than three vaguely sketched ships round out the tableau. Everything seems to indicate that, following an original composition including pentimenti, the artist wished to test his skills with a more ambitious arrangement that in the end appears looser and more clumsily structured.

The other two much larger versions show the same adolescent cut at mid-thigh but from a much closer angle than in the first version, that is, almost filling the surface of the canvas. The National Gallery of Canada version, dated 1867, places the flutist against a plain backdrop, while the other, dated the following year, again sets the musician in front of a body of water, this time with two boats, a hazy sun on the horizon, and a new addition—a pigeon in the left foreground. A fifth and final untraced variation, also dated 1868 and nearly square in shape, shows the flute player sitting in an armchair in an empty interior.

According to certain historiographic traditions, the Musée national des beaux-arts du Québec version of *The Flutist* was completed in 1855 and depicts Siméon Alary, Plamondon's assistant, playing a sunrise serenade to sailors of the French military ship *La Capricieuse*, anchored off Neuville. In response to criticism, the painting was supposedly modified and cut off at the bottom in 1866, hence the new date. While an in-depth examination of the painting completely contradicts this allegation, it is plausible that the figure is indeed Alary, who worked for the artist for some twelve years. His association with the Neuville painter is also corroborated by the 1871 census, in which he is recorded as a 21-year-old painting student. This would confirm the identity of the adolescent in the 1866 version, when Siméon was about fifteen.

The assertion that *La Capricieuse* is the ship in the background of the 1866 painting holds no water. In 1855, *La Capricieuse* was the first French warship to drop anchor in the St. Lawrence River since the Conquest. She was a pure sailing vessel, more specifically a first-class three-mast corvette—nothing like the one painted by Plamondon. Nor does Plamondon's ship bear any relation to *L'Admiral*, a two-mast steamer that the crew from *La Capricieuse* took to Montréal in July 1855, leaving the light frigate in Québec City. To convince the sceptics, we might add that the ship appearing in the 1866 version is a three-mast, mixed-propulsion vessel operating on both sail and steam power, as indicated by the red spot of the smokestack between the foremast and mainmast! We would also note that

the second and final versions contain up to three ships with no further identifying marks or resemblance to *La Capricieuse* or *L'Admiral*. Last, why would Plamondon, who never depicted contemporary Québec events in his paintings—unlike Légaré and Hamel—want to highlight the passage of *La Capricieuse* eleven years after the fact? Obviously, history enthusiasts longing for picturesque illustrations will have to live without Plamondon's supposed contribution to the legend of *La Capricieuse*!

Another tradition would equate the National Gallery of Canada version, signed "Québec, Canada," with the Plamondon "genre painting" that was listed in the 1867 Paris World's Fair catalogue and received an honourable mention at the event. Yet, contrary to the works of Théophile Hamel and Napoléon Bourassa, also exhibited in the Canadian section, no painting by Plamondon is mentioned in the newspaper articles, lists, and reports published during the 1867 World's Fair. In all likelihood, "Québec, Canada" would refer instead to the creation that year of the new province and Confederation.

Cat. 34
The Flutist
1866
Oil on canvas, 55 x 43.2 cm
Signed and dated lower left: Ant. Plamondon / 1866
Musée national des beaux-arts du Québec, acquired before 1934 (34.504)
Conservation treatment by the Centre de conservation du Québec

Cat. 35
The Flutist
Around 1866
Oil on canvas, 69.3 x 88.4 cm
Power Corporation du Canada / Power Corporation of Canada, Montréal

Be that as it may, the evolution of theme in *The Flutist* clearly reflects the artist's halting stops and starts in 1866, with many errors in perspective, shortcuts, and proportions which give way to a more adept positioning of the model in 1867 and 1868. The dramatic dawn light, with its colours exaggerated against the landscape, and the tall, slender subject, are ultimately softened by diffuse and neutral interior lighting in the National Gallery of Canada version, which is considered the most proficient. In short, we have moved from a Romanesque, anecdotal scene to a spare composition more akin to the art of portraiture than to that of genre painting.

Cat. 36
The Flutist
1867
Oil on canvas, 108.2 x 85.8 cm
Signed and dated lower right: Ant. Plamondon, p.xit 1867 / Québec, Canada.
National Gallery of Canada, Ottawa, purchased in 1973 (17605)

Cat. 37
The Flutist
1868
Oil on canvas, 106.5 x 84 cm
Signed and dated lower right: A. Plamondon / 1868.
Private collection, Toronto

Variations on a Still Life

Around age 65, Plamondon painted at least five still lifes from the same large Medicean vase filled with fruit, the significant variations between them proving beyond a shadow of a doubt that each is an original composition. Four versions are dated successively. The first, belonging to the Archdiocese of Ottawa, is dated 1868; the second, housed at the Musée national des beaux-arts du Québec, is dated 1869; and two similar versions in the collections of the Art Gallery of Windsor and The Montréal Museum of Fine Arts are dated 1870. A fifth, undated version housed at the National Gallery of Canada and derived directly from the 1870 composition, is almost square in shape, the artist having eliminated the lower portion illustrating the urn base and marble table. Note that in September 1871, Plamondon presented "two fruit paintings" at the Québec provincial exhibition—probably two of these variations. In 1880, the Neuville painter used the same vase to create a very different sixth version (destroyed in a fire) in which the fruit is replaced by a large bouquet of mixed flowers.

Apart from the first version, which is inscribed at the bottom left, all versions are ostensibly signed and dated on the base of the urn. This simple composition around a beautiful Medicean vase that stands out against a neutral backdrop includes variations in the play of light and vantage point, as well as in the positioning of the apples, grape bunches, and vine leaves. The very first 1868 version has no vine leaves, while the 1869 version includes, at the centre of the round table, three shiny cherries creating a repoussoir effect, drawing attention to the signature. In this last version, the artist also laid very thin, smooth layers of paint on a clear canvas base coat in order to highlight the transparent effect.

Did Plamondon work from photographs for his still lifes, as he did during the same period for portraits? We don't know. In this series, the painter studies front and plan views of the fruit arrangements and the balance between the solid objects placed carefully in the bowl or on the table, as well as lighting source and direction, with the vase placed in shadow or in harsh or diffuse light. In short, this fine academic composition of captivating naturalism and convincing realism plays on the tactile illusion of volume, material, and texture, as well as the effect of the highlights that caress the half-wilted leaves and satiny skin of fresh fruit, not to mention the translucent lustre of the alabaster vase and the cold polish of the veined marble table.

In 1880, Plamondon—who apparently was more than a little proud of his work—submitted the truncated version of his *Still Life with Apples and Grapes* as a diploma piece to the Royal Canadian Academy of Arts, of which he had just been named founding Vice President and honourary member.

Cat. 38
Still Life with Apples and Grapes
1868
Oil on canvas, 90.5 x 69.2 cm
Signed and dated lower left: A. Plamondon / 1868
L'Archidiocèse d'Ottawa / The Archdiocese of Ottawa

Cat. 39
Still Life with Apples and Grapes
1869
Oil on canvas, 98.4 x 77.5 cm
Signed and dated bottom centre (on the urn base): A. Plamondon. 1869
Musée national des beaux-arts du Québec,
gift of Mr. Maurice Corbeil (77.23)
Conservation treatment by the Centre de conservation du Québec

Cat. 40
Still Life with Apples and Grapes
1870
Oil on canvas, 97.7 x 77.5 cm
Signed and dated bottom centre (on the urn base): A. Plamondon / 1870
Art Gallery of Windsor,
gift of Mr. and Mrs. Norman A. McCormick, 1966 (1966.001)

Like most of his contemporaries, Plamondon took advantage of the commemorative movement that swept Québec around 1870. While Plamondon painted a naive *Duchesse d'Aiguillon* for Hôtel-Dieu de Québec as early as 1832, with the popularity of the historic portrait starting in the mid-19th century, he used older portraits to copy a number of famous figures from distant and mythical New France: around 1850, a *Marguerite Bourgeoys* (1620–1700) for the Congrégation Notre-Dame de Montréal, as well as a *Père Charlevoix* (1682–1761) for the stateroom of a steamship (destroyed by fire in the early 1850s); in 1851, a *Mgr de Laval* (1623–1708) for the Séminaire de Québec; and in 1879 a *Mgr Bailly de Messein* (1740–1794) for his adoptive parish. The portrait of Marie-Marguerite Dufrost de la Jemmerais (1701–1771), known as Mother d'Youville and founder of Hôpital Général de Montréal and the Sisters of Charity (Grey Nuns) congregation, certainly ties in with this patriotic celebration of New France notables.

An in-depth examination and meticulous research some fifteen years ago revealed that this painting apparently signed in Montréal in 1792 by François Malepart de Beaucourt (1740–1794) is actually a late 19th century copy of an old portrait housed at the Grey Nuns' Hôpital Général de Montréal. This portrait was itself inspired by a posthumous watercolour completed by Philippe Liébert (1733–1804) in 1771 showing Mother d'Youville on her deathbed. Beaucourt's painting, now a veritable community-revered relic, gave rise to a number of versions painted and engraved throughout the 19th century, including by Plamondon himself.

The Grey Nun archives indicate that in June 1873, "Mr. de Boucherville, to whom we lent the portrait of our Mother d'Youville, returned it together with a painting on canvas of Saint John the Evangelist, which he donated to the community." This painting (a gift to the MMFA in 2004), signed and dated by Plamondon in 1871, is similar in treatment and colouring to our *Mère d'Youville* which, according to Gérard Morisset, "comes from the de Boucherville family, related to the Dufrost

de la Jemmerais family." Everything seems to indicate that this "Mr. de Boucherville" asked Plamondon to produce a literal copy of the famous Grey Nun portrait in addition to a *Saint John the Evangelist* after Le Dominiquin. At the client's request, or to distance himself from the awkwardness of his required model, Plamondon went so far as to imitate Beaucourt's usual penmanship—now hidden under thick layers of paint—while using a broader stroke and warmer colours, in keeping with the tastes of the day.

Cat. 41
Mère d'Youville, after François Malepart de Beaucourt
Around 1873
Oil on canvas, 75.8 x 60.5 cm
Signed and dated lower left and right: F. Beaucourt, pinxit A Montréal, 1792.
Musée national des beaux-arts du Québec, purchase (56.421)

After Saint Cecilia *by Raphael*

Plamondon's religious production consists mainly of copies of Old European Masters. Of all the 16th and 17th century French and Italian artists Plamondon copied, Raphael was probably his favourite. While he was especially captivated by Madonnas, as we see in "*La Belle Jardinière*" of the Musée national des beaux-arts du Québec (1878), Plamondon was also interested in other compositions by the grand master of the Italian High Renaissance, particularly the famous *Saint Cecilia* of the Pinacoteca Nazionale in Bologna (1514–1516), also a cherished subject in the Victorian era.

After training in Paris between 1826 and 1830, Plamondon returned to Canada with a first *Saint Cecilia* based on an engraving or another French copy, since the original painting was in Italy at the time. Unless, of course, this copy confirms Georges Bellerive's 1925 claim that the young artist traveled to Italy to copy several masterpieces after finishing his studies in France. Whatever the case may be, the Québec painter used his practice copy to produce two large versions for the parishes of Sainte-Cécile du Bic in 1857 and Saint-Jean-Baptiste de Québec in 1869 (both versions were destroyed in fires). The latter earned him an "epigram" in *Le Courrier du Canada* and election as an honourary member of the Union musicale. In 1872, he signed three small paintings, probably for private commissions, limited to the saint's bust (MAFQ, Agnes Etherington Art Centre in Kingston, and unknown location). Six years later, Plamondon delivered a final large version that was housed at Saint-Dominique church in Québec City before being added to our collection.

Plamondon greatly simplified Raphael's composition while using his own colours for most of the decor. He limited the scene to the main character, removing the four secondary figures and celestial choir of cherubs, and reducing the musical instruments set on the ground to the viola de gamba and one kettledrum. Note that the second kettledrum, which seeps through and is therefore still visible, was painted out of the original composition. Set in an expansive ancient Roman landscape, the patron saint of musicians is still easily recognizable thanks to her tiny inverted portable organ. Her eyes lifted heavenward, the virgin martyr listens in ecstasy to the angels' sacred song. Himself a musician, Plamondon must have been highly sensitive to the subject, as in 1884 he contributed half the funds to purchase a Déry organ for his parish, provided he be allowed to play a piece "each Sunday during the high mass."

Cat. 42 (next page)
Saint Cecilia, after Raphael
1878
Oil on canvas, 184 x 113.5 cm
Signed and dated lower left: A. Plamondon / 1878
Musée national des beaux-arts du Québec,
gift of the Fabrique de Saint-Dominique de Québec (73.568)
Conservation treatment by the Centre de conservation du Québec

Portraits from Photos

In March 1871, Plamondon published an ad in the Québec City newspapers offering to paint portraits from good quality photographs (see fig. 14). He probably used this common practice of many contemporary portrait painters to produce the picture of an unidentified man dated 1878, most likely one of his fellow Neuville parishioners, many of whom posed for him at the time. According to Plamondon's ad, this small portrait including only the model's "head, shoulders, and chest" fell into the category of "simple busts." Despite its photographic realism, the man's head seems mismatched with his barrel-chested body, lending the subject a false air of grandeur. Note that contrary to Théophile Hamel, for example, Plamondon does not seem to have indicated that his portraits were painted from photos.

What is certain is that Plamondon used still another photograph four years later for his famous *Self Portrait*, in which he is seated at a table with a palette and brushes in plain view. In this case the source is clearly known—a medallion cabinet portrait stamped by Québec City's reputable Livernois studio, managed by Jules-Ernest Livernois since December 1873. Our albumenized paper print was signed and dated by the painter in 1874 at "age 71." Bear in mind that Plamondon was born on February 29, 1804.

On the painting signed and dated 1882, Plamondon—according to a common practice at the end of his career—ostensibly noted his age as 80, now making himself two years older! Contrary to the photo dated eight years earlier, the painting now shows a rejuvenated old man who has traded his jacket for a greatcoat that gives him sloping shoulders. The head is still massive, but clearly cosmetically enhanced—a less chiselled face with a wide, bare forehead is framed by a long, white, better-trimmed beard; the features are softened with darker blue eyes that have lost the steely gaze in the photo that left the observer cold. Affable despite himself, the elderly man has become almost likeable—although known for his rather difficult nature! It is also interesting to note that the painter is seated at a table, a positioning that shares some similarity with Titian's *Young Woman at the Mirror*. Plamondon's late-career *Self Portrait* thus echoes his copy of Titian's painting made when he was a student in Paris (see cat. 1). The photographic portrait of 1874 and the idealized *Self Portrait* of 1882 also appear to be linked in that they both eloquently illustrate the relationship between photography and painting in the artist.

That said, the gallery of photographic portraits and self portraits painted by Plamondon would not be complete without the *Self Portrait* painted in Paris in 1827 (see fig. 3) and the visiting card portrait made around 1860 (see fig.12), again at the Livernois studio, in two slightly different angles showing the artist from top to bottom, seated in a sculpted armchair. 1827, 1860, 1874, 1882: four periods in a life, four milestones in a remarkable artistic journey marked by affirmation and adaptation.

Cat. 43
Portrait of a Man
1878
Oil on canvas, 63.4 x 52.7 cm
Signed and dated centre left: Plamondon / 1878
Musée national des beaux-arts du Québec, purchase (84.22)
Conservation treatment by the Centre de conservation du Québec

Cat. 45
Jules-Ernest Livernois (Québec City, 1851–1933)
Antoine Plamondon
1874
Original albumen silver print, paper on cardboard,
16.1 x 11 cm (cabinet card format)
Stamped on card at bottom of photo: J. E. Livernois, Photo. Quebec.
Handwritten in ink at bottom of photo: Ant. Plamondon. peintre,
1874 / <u>71 ans</u>.
Musée national des beaux-arts du Québec, purchase (2005.15)

Cat. 44
Self Portrait
1882
Oil on canvas, 82.2 x 65.2 cm
Signed and dated lower right: A. Plamondon. 1882. / (80 ans.)
Musée de la civilisation, Séminaire de Québec Collection (1991.101)

A. Plamondon. 1882.
(80 ans.)

Appendices

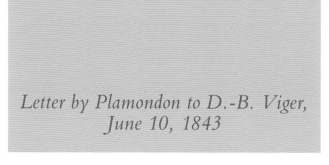
In 1838, Plamondon had in his possession a Rubens School painting, *The Beheading of Saint John the Baptist*, that actually corresponds to *The Feast of Herod* from the Desjardins collection housed some ten years previously by the Ursuline Sisters of Québec City. During a visit to the painter's new studio, journalist and draughtsman Napoléon Aubin (1812–1890) was particularly captivated by this painting then available for purchase, as indicated in his review published in Québec City's *Le Fantasque* on July 28, 1838. At the very end of the year, Plamondon announced in *L'Affiche* that he still had "a magnificent painting by Rubens." Five years later, in a letter dated June 10, 1843, the artist again tried to sell his painting, this time to Montréal politician and avid art collector Denis-Benjamin Viger (see cat. 27 and 33), penning a description as colourful as it was flawed:

I am taking the liberty of writing to you to inform you that I have within my studio an authentic painting by the famous P.P. Rubens, which is seven-and-a-half feet wide and four feet nine inches high. The subject is the Beheading of St. John the Baptist, or Herod's Feast. At dessert, the venerable head is brought in a basin before the miserable King, who blanches and, with his left hand, tries to push away the bloodied head which seems to still be reproaching him for his crimes and, especially, the horrible assassination freshly committed by him. Twenty one persons around the table of the murderous King jostle to see the head of he who came so courageously to trouble their vile conscience, a few figures are on the verge of drunkenness, others seem terrified to see the head of this great Prophet cut off at the bidding of their master and brought to his table at the end of a meal!!! This beautiful painting, this splendid composition, this lovely study for those engaged in this divine art of painting, it must be sold shortly [...] I felt I must tell you, since you would surely be right to rebuke me severely if I had allowed this painting to slip into the hands of strangers, that would be so fitting in a Canadian house, the most beautiful work of art one can see, and unique in this country. It would be truly vexing if a Canadian household did not acquire it. This painting would be very costly in Europe. However, to hasten its sale in this country, I am letting it go for one hundred louis only. If you do us the honour of a visit, perhaps you will find this painting by Rubens to be worthwhile. In the meantime, I remain most respectfully, Sir, your humble and obedient Servant,

Ant. Plamondon, Painter.

This offer was also unsuccessful, as two years later, on August 18, 1845, after a fire that damaged his workshop on June 28, the painter announced in the Québec City newspaper *Le Canadien* that he "was obliged to part with" his small but precious collection, which still included a Rubens. The painting's subsequent fate is uncertain.

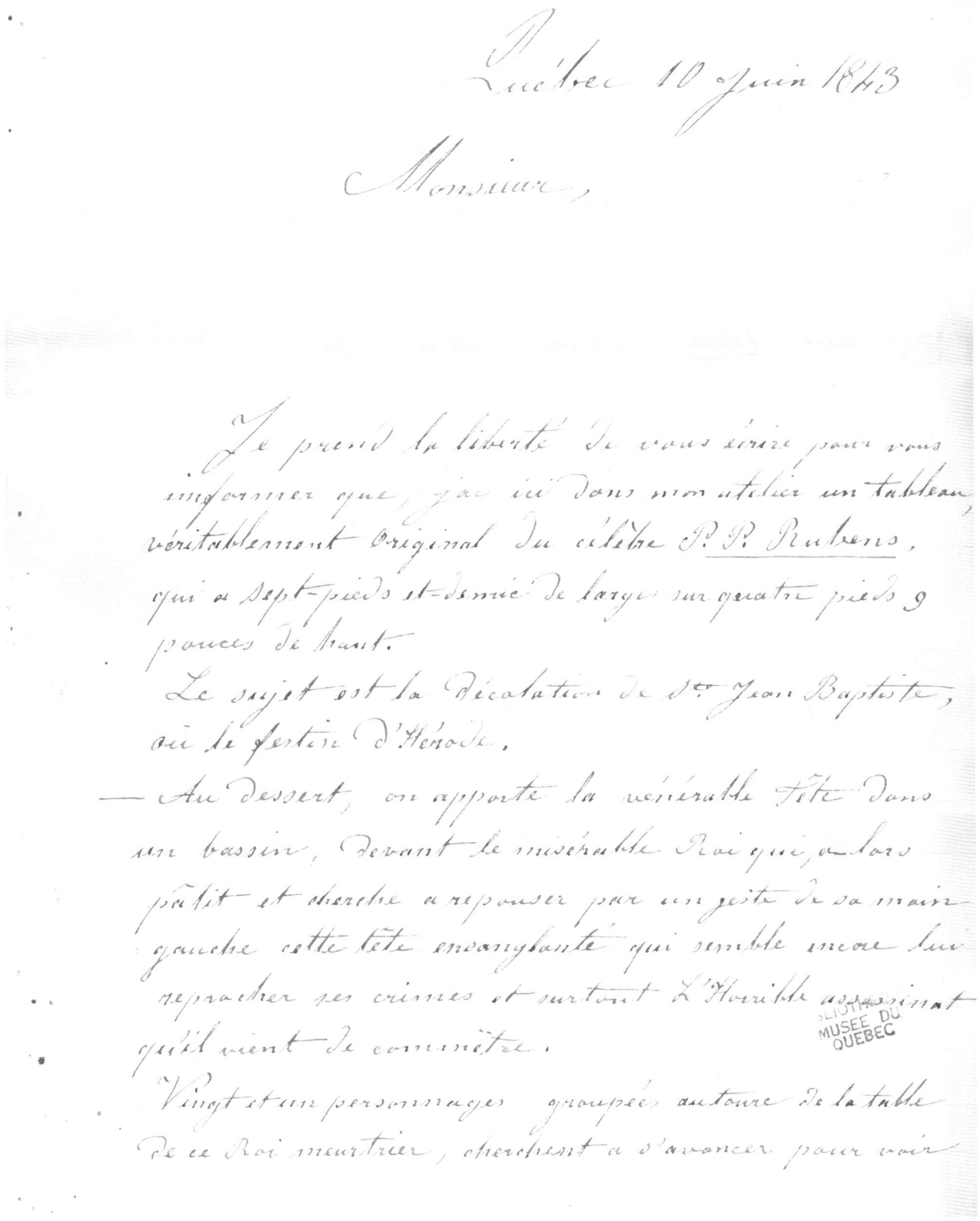

Québec 10 juin 1843

Monsieur,

Je prend la liberté de vous écrire pour vous informer que, j'ai ici dans mon atelier un tableau véritablement Original du célèbre P.P. Rubens, qui a sept-pieds et demie de large sur quatre pieds 9 pouces de haut.

Le sujet est la Décolation de St. Jean Baptiste, ou le festin d'Hérode.

— Au dessert, on apporte la vénérable Tête dans un bassin, devant le misérable Roi qui, a lors palit et cherche a repouser par un geste de sa main gauche cette Tête ensanglanté qui semble encore lui reprocher ses crimes et surtout L'Horrible assassinat qu'il vient de commêtre.

Vingt et un personnages groupées autour de la table de ce Roi meurtrier, cherchent a s'avancer pour voir

Fig. 21
Letter from Antoine Plamondon to the Honourable Denis-Benjamin Viger (1774–1861) dated June 10, 1843, offering to sell *The Beheading of Saint John the Baptist* attributed to Rubens. Bibliothèque du Musée national des beaux-arts du Québec, Québec City.

Plamondon and the Question of Drawing

Until very recently, the Musée national des beaux-arts du Québec had a good number of drawings attributed to Antoine Plamondon, most on the basis of the simple initials "A.P.," a type of overly discreet signature that the vain artist seldom used on his paintings. These initials are certainly consistent in their placement—often on the right above the shoulder—and handwriting, with letters similar to the signatures on Plamondon's paintings, but with numbers that are too careful and dissimilar not to raise doubts. Certainly, no Canadian portrait painters who were contemporaries of Plamondon had the initials "A.P." A study of the literature and an in-depth examination of the works have helped unearth certain facts, separate truth from falsehood, and thereby lead to a better understanding of Plamondon as a draughtsman.

First, these drawings (all portraits except for one hunting scene) were made using a variety of techniques including pencil, charcoal—sometimes with chalk or gouache highlights—and even watercolour, a medium Plamondon never used, to our knowledge. In addition, most of these drawings, acquired primarily from Montréal merchants on the cusp of the 1970s, have no information on source or history. Consequently, most of the portrait models are not identified. In addition, the arrangement of subjects is often nothing like Plamondon's usual approach, whether for a medallion, a double portrait, or a model in profile or who is not looking at the observer. One of these drawings was even determined to be a lithograph to which the initials "A.P." had intentionally been added! And what can be said of the whimsical hunting scene in the European tradition, which raised a number of doubts and questions as to its authenticity (fig. 22) in the past? In short, no correspondence in technique, form, or style can be identified among all these drawings, some of which may even be from Europe (fig. 23) or copies of engravings. The same is true of the other drawings with the same famous initials housed in Canadian collections or put on the market since the 1960s.

Of the dozen at the Musée national des beaux-arts du Québec examined initially, only three are proven works by Plamondon, all three signed and dated 1863. Along with these is a charcoal drawing on paper glued on canvas dated 1834, unfortunately in very poor condition, deposited in the Musée collection by the Archives nationales du Québec. It may be useful to note that Plamondon was a drawing instructor at the Séminaire de Québec for at least seven years—from 1833 to 1835, then from 1840 to 1845—as well as at the Sainte-Anne-de-la-Pocatière college in 1833 and Hôpital Général de Québec in 1841, which at least confirms his knowledge and regular practice, if not his talent.

The Archives nationales du Québec portrait (fig. 24) is dated 1834, the same year as Plamondon's first stint at the Séminaire. It is therefore hardly surprising that he should draw a pupil, in this instance 17-year-old Honoré Tanguay (1817–1862), who studied at the Séminaire from 1825 to 1834. Honoré was the brother of Cyprien, whom Plamondon captured in a superb oil portrait two years earlier (see cat. 2). The adolescent, with his fine and delicate features and slightly slanted eyes, is shown wearing the official Séminaire uniform—a dark jacket with white piping adorned with a wide tie belt and a handsome Windsor tie. The subject's placement is entirely consistent with that of neoclassically inspired oil portraits of the early 1830s (see cat. 4 to 6).

The three other Musée national des beaux-arts du Québec drawings, made in charcoal and pencil, bear fairly revelatory ink inscriptions at the bottom. It is interesting to note that in 1863, Plamondon still called himself a "history painter." Successively dated February 16, May 6, and June 21, 1863, the portraits respectively depict Charles Huot, a 40 year-old teacher; Marie Josephte Racette, age 58; and her husband, Joseph Juneau, age 52 (fig. 25), a farmer in Saint-Augustin-de-Portneuf. Drawing largely from photographs, these portraits certainly show careful execution, but are not without a certain stiffness or even hardness and dryness in stroke. These four large unpublished charcoal drawings give us a glimpse into Plamondon's art as a draughtsman at two disparate points in his career, that is, his beginnings in Québec City and some 12 years after he settled in Neuville.

Fig. 22
Unknown artist, *Hunting Scene*, 1863; charcoal on paper, 38.7 x 45 cm; signed and dated lower left (on the rock): AP / 1863.
Musée national des beaux-arts du Québec, purchase (68.263).

Fig. 23
Unknown artist, *Young Woman*, 1852; charcoal on paper, 36.5 x 27.8 cm; signed and dated lower right: A.P. / 1852.
Musée national des beaux-arts du Québec, purchase (71.77).

Fig. 24
Honoré Tanguay; April 1834; charcoal on paper glued on canvas, 19 x 48.5 cm; signed and dated in ink on the reverse side of the canvas:
H. Tanguay. 17 ans. / Ant: Plamondon Fecit / Avril 1834. Musée national des beaux-arts du Québec, Archives nationales du Québec deposit, Québec City.

Fig. 25
Joseph Juneau, 1863; charcoal and pencil on paper, 67.7 x 52.7 cm; signed in ink, bottom centre: Joseph Juneau, agé de 52 ans, le / 21 Juin, 1863 / Defsiné par M. Ant Plamondon, Peintre d'histoire. Musée national des beaux-arts du Québec, purchase (77.17).

Selective Bibliography

A nearly exhaustive bibliography on Antoine Plamondon accompanies John R. Porter's article published in 1990 in the *Dictionary of Canadian Biography*. Another worthwhile source is *Painting in Québec 1820-1850*, published two years later.

- Mario BÉLAND, edited by, *Painting in Québec 1820-1850. New Views, New Perspectives* (cat.), Québec City, Musée du Québec, 1992, 605 p. Essays by John R. Porter, Paul Bourassa and Laurier Lacroix, and notes (22 works) by them and by Yves Lacasse, Mario Béland and Joanne Chagnon.

- *Les Chemins de la mémoire*, Tome III, *Biens mobiliers du Québec*, Québec City, Commission des biens culturels du Québec / Les Publications du Québec, 1999, 428 p.

- Robert H. HUBBARD, *Deux peintres de Québec / Two Painters of Quebec : Antoine Plamondon/1804-1895, Théophile Hamel/ 1817-1870* (cat.), Ottawa, The National Gallery of Canada, 1970, 176 p.

- David KAREL, *Dictionnaire des artistes de langue française en Amérique du Nord*, Québec City, Musée du Québec and Les Presses de l'Université Laval, 1992, pp. 643-647.

- Yves LACASSE, *Antoine Plamondon (1804-1895). The Way of the Cross of the Church of Notre-Dame de Montréal* (cat.), The Montreal Museum of Fine Arts, 1984, 111 p., completed, by the same author, by « La source gravée de *L'Agonie au jardin des Oliviers* d'Antoine Plamondon (1804-1895) », *The Journal of Canadian Art History*, Vol. X, No. 1 (1987), pp. 42-47.

- Gérard MORISSET, *Peintres et tableaux*, Québec City, Les éditions du Chevalet, 1936-1937, Vol. 1, pp. 141-207; Vol. 2, pp. 117-154 (Les arts au Canada français).

- Gérard MORISSET, *La peinture traditionnelle au Canada français*, Ottawa, Le Cercle du livre de France, 1960, pp. 103-112.

- Rémi MORISSETTE, *Antoine Plamondon et ses peintures dans l'église de Neuville*, La Société d'histoire de Neuville, 2004, 31 p. (« Les cahiers neuvillois », No. 9).

- John R. PORTER, *Antoine Plamondon. Sister Saint-Alphonse*, Ottawa, The National Gallery of Canada, 1975, 32 p. ("Masterpieces in the National Gallery of Canada," No. 4).

- John R. PORTER, « Antoine Plamondon (1804-1895) et le tableau religieux : perception et valorisation de la copie et de la composition », *The Journal of Canadian Art History*, Vol. VIII, No. 1 (1984), pp. 1-25.

- John R. PORTER, "Plamondon, Antoine," *Dictionary of Canadian Biography*, Vol. XII (1891 to 1900), University of Toronto Press, 1990, pp. 845-853.